BARRON'S

G000160691

FYODOR DOSTOEVSKY'S
Crime and Punishment

BY

Virginia B. Morris
Associate Professor of English
John Jay College, City University of New York

SERIES EDITOR

Michael Spring
Editor, *Literary Cavalcade*
Scholastic Inc.

BARRON'S EDUCATIONAL SERIES, INC.
Woodbury, New York / London / Toronto / Sydney

For Ralph and Dorothea Baumgartner

ACKNOWLEDGMENTS

We would like to acknowledge the many painstaking hours of work Holly Hughes and Thomas F. Hirsch have devoted to making the *Book Notes* series a success.

All inquiries should be addressed to:
Barron's Educational Series, Inc.
113 Crossways Park Drive
Woodbury, New York 11797

International Standard Book No. 0-8120-3409-0

PRINTED IN THE UNITED STATES OF AMERICA

456   550   987654321

CONTENTS

ADVISORY BOARD

HOW TO USE THIS BOOK

You have to know how to approach literature in order to get the most out of it. This *Barron's Book Notes* volume follows a plan based on methods used by some of the best students to read a work of literature.

Begin with the guide's section on the author's life and times. As you read, try to form a clear picture of the author's personality, circumstances, and motives for writing the work. This background usually will make it easier for you to hear the author's tone of voice, and follow where the author is heading.

Then go over the rest of the introductory material—such sections as those on the plot, characters, setting, themes, and style of the work. Underline, or write down in your notebook, particular things to watch for, such as contrasts between characters and repeated literary devices. At this point, you may want to develop a system of symbols to use in marking your text as you read. (Of course, you should only mark up a book you own, not one that belongs to another person or a school.) Perhaps you will want to use a different letter for each character's name, a different number for each major theme of the book, a different color for each important symbol or literary device. Be prepared to mark up the pages of your book as you read. Put your marks in the margins so you can find them again easily.

Now comes the moment you've been waiting for—the time to start reading the work of literature. You may want to put aside your *Barron's Book Notes* volume until you've read the work all the way through. Or you may want to alternate, reading the

Book Notes analysis of each section as soon as you have finished reading the corresponding part of the original. Before you move on, reread crucial passages you don't fully understand. (Don't take this guide's analysis for granted—make up your own mind as to what the work means.)

Once you've finished the whole work of literature, you may want to review it right away, so you can firm up your ideas about what it means. You may want to leaf through the book concentrating on passages you marked in reference to one character or one theme. This is also a good time to reread the *Book Notes* introductory material, which pulls together insights on specific topics.

When it comes time to prepare for a test or to write a paper, you'll already have formed ideas about the work. You'll be able to go back through it, refreshing your memory as to the author's exact words and perspective, so that you can support your opinions with evidence drawn straight from the work. Patterns will emerge, and ideas will fall into place; your essay question or term paper will almost write itself. Give yourself a dry run with one of the sample tests in the guide. These tests present both multiple-choice and essay questions. An accompanying section gives answers to the multiple-choice questions as well as suggestions for writing the essays. If you have to select a term paper topic, you may choose one from the list of suggestions in this book. This guide also provides you with a reading list, to help you when you start research for a term paper, and a selection of provocative comments by critics, to spark your thinking before you write.

THE AUTHOR AND HIS TIMES

When Fyodor Dostoevsky was twenty-eight, he was arrested by the Czar's secret police and sentenced to death, along with other members of a group that supported revolutionary political and social ideas. (His particular crime was publishing illegal articles advocating changes in Russian society.) When the prisoners were bound and waiting to be shot, and as the Czar's firing squad readied for the execution, a royal messenger dramatically announced a reprieve. The men's lives were spared.

The spectacular salvation had been prearranged. The Czar had merely wanted to frighten the men and demonstrate his power. Dostoevsky got the message. More important, his escape from death—followed by four years of imprisonment in Siberia—had an enormous impact on his life and work.

When you read Dostoevsky's novels, it's easy to see how his experiences influenced his choice of theme and character. This is especially true of *Crime and Punishment*, published in 1867, which tells the story of a brilliant but emotionally tortured young man whose theories about human behavior make him think he is above the law. At the end of Part Two of the novel, for example, Raskolnikov, the main character, suddenly feels "a boundlessly full and powerful life welling up in him." He compares the emotion to the reaction of "a man condemned to death and unexpectedly reprieved." The source and significance of that image are overwhelmingly clear.

Dostoevsky's prison experience provoked his interest in the causes of crime. It also made him wonder about the usefulness of punishment. In a letter describing his plan to write *Crime and Punishment*, he said, "Punishment meted out by the law to the criminal deters the criminal far less than the lawgivers think. . . ." He believed that in order for punishment to work, it had to make the criminal accept his own guilt. His ideas about rehabilitating criminals were far ahead of the accepted attitudes of his time.

Another of Dostoevsky's innovative attitudes about crime and punishment was his emphasis on the emotional or psychological reasons why people commit crimes. In his time social scientists had only begun to use emotional factors as an explanation for changes in people's behavior. The field of criminology, which studies the various causes of crime, was not clearly formulated until about 1910.

There are other experiences in Dostoevsky's life that are important to understanding *Crime and Punishment*. At seventeen he left home to study engineering in a military school in St. Petersburg (now called Leningrad). He was miserable there, partly because he was really more interested in literature than in science. Also, incredible poverty plagued his student life. Often he went hungry, and he knew all about pawnbrokers as a poor man's only source of money. He frequented taverns and was acquainted with the seedy part of life in the city. The stifling, poverty-stricken slums and the teeming, drunken crowds in the Haymarket Square section of St. Petersburg are so vividly described in *Crime and Punishment* because he knew them from personal experience. From the beginning Dostoevsky's fiction depicted desperately poor men and women.

Dostoevsky's fascination with doubling—the psychological term to describe dual personalities—is one of the reasons he's often described as one of the first modern novelists. Characters with double personalities exist in many old legends and tales, but his analysis of such characters as emotionally, and often mentally, disturbed was provocative and influential. In fact, *Crime and Punishment* is still used in psychology lectures to illustrate the phenomenon of split personalities.

You can understand even more about the ideas that obsessed Dostoevsky if you know what happened to his father. At about the time Dostoevsky moved to St. Petersburg, his father, with whom he'd never been close, was murdered by the outraged serfs on his country estate. Many readers, searching for ways to explain some of the emotional instability in the author's own life, point to this murder as a key influence. Fathers aren't ever depicted very positively in his work; in *Crime and Punishment* the only father we see is a bad one.

Scholars who've written about Dostoevsky often suggest a connection between the epileptic seizures that began to plague him in the 1840s and his father's death. In *Crime and Punishment* the novelist himself suggests a connection between emotional problems and physical illness; it would be fascinating to know if he saw his own illness as psychologically based.

The period of Russian history in which Dostoevsky lived and wrote was tumultuous. New ideas for change were in the air, as his own early political ideas illustrate. Russian serfs were freed in 1861. Many Russian thinkers believed that their nation should forge closer ties with Western Europe and become "modern," an idea Dostoevsky rejected.

Believers in Nihilism, one of the most influential movements of the period, preached the need to destroy the existing social and political systems even if nothing had been set up to replace what was destroyed. Dostoevsky, after his prison experience, was repelled by this negative view of life, even though its advocates offered some constructive ideas for reform.

Another idea that was in the air was that of the "superman," an extraordinary individual set apart from most other men. The German philosopher Georg Friedrich Hegel had written a great deal on the subject, and his countryman Friedrich Wilhelm Nietzsche developed the idea in different ways during the 1880s. Hegel suggested that a superman works for the good of mankind, whereas Nietzsche's idea was that a superman was primarily interested in self-gratification. The character Raskolnikov in *Crime and Punishment* uses the idea of the superman to help justify the murder he commits. Dostoevsky challenges us to weigh Raskolnikov's ideas against the seriousness of his crime and draw our own conclusions.

Dostoevsky's fascination with suffering is based on his religious beliefs—fervent but not always orthodox Christianity. Christian ideas of forgiveness, salvation, and rebirth (or resurrection) of the spirit are also central to *Crime and Punishment*.

The novel is exciting to read because Dostoevsky makes these ideas come alive in a suspenseful story. As you read the novel, you'll be challenged to form your own opinions about contradictory views of human behavior. Does Dostoevsky want us to agree with Raskolnikov that some people have the right to commit crimes? There are times when you think he does, and other times when you're sure he doesn't.

THE NOVEL

The Plot

Rodion Romanovich Raskolnikov is a desperate man. He thinks he's exceptional, extraordinary. He believes that gives him the right to break the law if he chooses. But he's also a physical and emotional wreck, afraid to do the things he wants to do to test his own courage.

Driven by his poverty and the shame of his mother's and sister's sacrifices for him, he plans a bold act: to kill a repulsive old pawnbroker. Her murder will accomplish two things: give him the money he needs and prove he's a superman. The plan misfires. He kills not only his intended victim but also her mild, gentle sister, who returns home too early and surprises the murderer.

Made physically ill by the trauma of his deed, Raskolnikov is cared for by his old friend Razumikhin. But his behavior becomes so bizarre that everyone who meets him wonders if he's insane. Unfortunately for him, several police officials, including Porfiry Petrovich, the investigator in charge of the pawnbroker's murder, hear about his self-incriminating actions. He faints in the police station when the crime is discussed; he returns to the scene of the crime and makes a spectacle of himself; and he is obsessed with the details of the murder. Even without any physical evidence against him, suspicion focuses on him.

The other side of Raskolnikov's personality, the side that feels sympathy for other people's troubles, finds an outlet in the midst of his own struggle to escape detection. He meets the family of Marmeladov, a drunk who is killed in a street accident; he's so appalled by the family's poverty that he gives them all his money to see them through the funeral. He's most intrigued by Marmeladov's daughter, Sonia, who has become a prostitute to bring in enough money to provide food and shelter.

To complicate Raskolnikov's problems, his mother and his sister, Dunya, arrive in St. Petersburg the same day Marmeladov dies. They have come to prepare for Dunya's wedding to the affluent but repulsive Luzhin. Dunya's former employer, Svidrigailov, a man who has tried to seduce her and is still eager to see her, also shows up at Raskolnikov's apartment. Raskolnikov feels increasingly tormented, but he still wants to go on living; he resists the temptation to kill himself and end his troubles.

Because Sonia Marmeladov is so forgiving and, at the same time, guilty herself of immoral acts, he decides that she is the only one in whom he can confide. He can't ignore Porfiry Petrovich either, though, because he knows that the investigator suspects him. Raskolnikov alternates visits with his confessor and his pursuer, both of whom force him to reexamine his behavior. Both Sonia and Porfiry talk to him about spiritual rebirth and want him to turn himself in to the police. They both believe he can be saved. He resists both of them.

Then he finds out that Svidrigailov has overheard his confessions to Sonia. Raskolnikov knows that such information, in court testimony, would confirm his guilt. What worries him even more is that the unscrupulous Svidrigailov will use his knowledge to blackmail Dunya into a physical relationship to protect her brother. Raskolnikov never hears about it, but Svidrigailov does exactly what he'd feared. Dunya resists his threats, however, and even tries to shoot him to protect her honor. Forced to face his own decadence and the fact that Dunya will never love him, Svidrigailov commits suicide.

Raskolnikov has been thinking about suicide again himself, but he's not ready to die. He decides that even the humiliation of a trial and the misery of prison are better than dying. But he also realizes that he can't go on living with the tension of trying to escape detection. He goes to Sonia for her blessing and then goes to the police.

His sentence is eight years in Siberia. At first he is as arrogant and self-involved as ever, but a miracle happens at Easter of his second year in prison. He recognizes that, if widely followed, the theories that led him to commit murder would doom the world to anarchy. In shedding his egotism, he is also able to recognize that he loves Sonia. Though their life together will have many hardships, they can believe in the promise of the future.

The Characters

Before you read *Crime and Punishment*, you should understand something about Russian names. Every character has a middle name called a *patronymic*, formed from his or her father's first name. For a man, the patronymic ends in *ovich;* for a woman, its ending is *ovna*. The patronymic is considered an important part of a name and is commonly used, unlike our own middle names.

The characters are also often identified by their nicknames, so it might take you a little while to realize that Rodya, Roddy, Rodka, and Rodenka all refer to Raskolnikov. It's a good idea to make a list, either inside the book or on an index card, of all the characters' names and their variations. Translators also use different spellings. Most of the variants are given in parentheses. The spellings used here are from David Margarshack's translation.

MAJOR CHARACTERS

Rodion Romanovich Raskolnikov (Rodya, Roddy, Rodenka, Rodka)

Is Raskolnikov a criminal who should be severely punished for his crime—or a tortured young man who makes a terrible mistake in trying to understand himself? Because his crime is so brutal, many readers think he's a repulsive, self-centered character who escapes the punishment he deserves. In contrast, because he's tormented by his conscience and full of pity for the needy, other readers feel that the murders were a dreadful mistake that should not ruin his life. Dostoevsky shows the reader both sides of Raskolnikov, but the structure of the novel supports the author's belief that Raskolnikov can be rehabilitated. The reader has to decide if Dostoevsky proves his point.

In choosing Raskolnikov's name, he has given one important clue to his character. The word *raskol*, in Russian, means "schism" or "split." Dualism is the key to Raskolnikov's character. He is torn between the desire to do evil and the desire to do good.

He wants to do evil, to commit murder, in order to test his theory that there is such a thing as a crime of principle. He believes he is brilliant and more gifted than other people and has the right to commit crime to accomplish his goals. All he needs is daring. The problem is, he's not exactly sure what his goals are.

He also wants to do good. He wants to save his sister from an unhappy marriage and his mother from sacrificing for him. He wants to help the miserable Marmeladov family. But he seems unable to motivate himself to work or to find a way to break out of the poverty that traps him.

He struggles constantly with self-doubt, questioning what he does and blaming himself for every decision he makes. He is tortured by dreams in which he must confront his own evil acts and guilty conscience. He constantly suggests new motives for his crime, and then rejects them. Dostoevsky attributes Raskolnikov's turmoil in part to his self-imposed isolation, which has warped his ability to cope with people. His friends think he is insane—or at least mentally unbalanced. But, according to how Dostoevsky finally wants us to see Raskolnikov, it is not insanity, but alienation from humanity and from Christian ethical standards that allows him to kill the pawnbroker.

After the murders, Raskolnikov's most important relationships are with Sonia Marmeladov and Porfiry Petrovich. At first he seeks out Sonia, the reluctant prostitute and devout Christian, because he can feel superior to her. To her he can confess his crime, and with her he can share his misery. Eventually she becomes his hope for salvation through her love for him.

As Sonia is his spiritual confessor, Porfiry Petrovich, the brilliant detective, is his intellectual equal. His heart seeks Sonia, but his mind seeks the challenge of sparring with Porfiry. Dostoevsky makes this pattern clear by contrasting each visit with Sonia with an interview with Porfiry. By having both of these characters more concerned with saving his soul than punishing his crime, the novelist also emphasizes the moral and religious dimensions of crime and punishment. According to Dostoevsky, the killer must recognize he has committed a sin against God and man before his punishment can work.

Raskolnikov finally does confess and is sent to prison. He has as many confused motives for confessing as he did for committing the crime in the first place. The most positive reason is that he recognizes he has done wrong and must be punished. But Dostoevsky suggests that physical and emotional exhaustion are equally a factor in his decision. The tension of constantly being on his guard finally drives him to give up. A third reason—that Svidrigailov's suicide shocks Raskolnikov into recognizing that unconfessed crime leads to despair and death—is also possible. He knows he doesn't want to die. Finally, many readers believe that Raskolnikov seeks punishment all along. That, they say, explains all the self-incriminating things he says and does after the murder, including all the times he starts to confess and is prevented from doing so.

NOTE: As you read the novel, other reasons for both Raskolnikov's crime and his confession will strike you too. Be sure to note passages in the novel that support your view of Raskolnikov's character. Several different reasons can be true at the same time, and Dostoevsky makes that very clear. Complicated people can never be explained in simple ways.

Sofya Semenovna Marmeladova (Sonia)

Sonia, whose name comes from the Greek word for wisdom, shows Raskolnikov the way to redemption. But she is a contradictory, or dual, character, too. Like some other women in literature, she is portrayed as a combination of the madonna and the whore, a woman whose soul is pure even though her body is defiled.

Sonia has become a prostitute because her father is a drunk, unable to support his family. But, miraculously, she seems untouched by her experience, although she acknowledges the brutal truth that life on the street has only three possible outcomes: suicide, madness, or corruption. It is because she is sinful that Raskolnikov is able to confide in her; but it is because she believes in God that she is able to help him.

She is in the best position to understand the split in his character, because she is intimately connected with both sides of it. He befriends her family at the time of her father's death, and he defends her against a false charge of theft. Yet he has killed her friend Lizaveta, the pawnbroker's sister, and he continually reminds her of the misery of her life and the uselessness of her sacrifice.

Dostoevsky stresses Sonia's belief in the power of suffering. She is fervent in her belief in God and trusts that he will reward her misery. If there will be positive results, she can tolerate her shame—perhaps even welcome it. The novel affirms her faith, at least to some extent. By the end of *Crime and Punishment*, Sonia's brother and sisters have been placed in a good orphanage; she is able to leave her life as a prostitute; and Raskolnikov repents and is redeemed.

Readers respond to Sonia in different ways. You may agree with those who think she is nearly perfect. The religious themes in the novel center around her, and she exemplifies perfect human love, which accepts others with all their failings and asks nothing in return. For example, she struggles to understand the complexity of Raskolnikov's inner turmoil and loves him anyway, even while he is cruel and uncaring to her.

If you find all her goodness rather cloying and unrealistic, however, you are not alone. Many readers think she's too good, too passive, too willing to suffer without complaint. She rarely exerts herself or insists on her rights. While Raskolnikov seems very modern in his anguish and alienation, Sonia seems old-fashioned and limited.

Remember that your personal reaction is only one part of evaluating a character. You also have to take into account what the author intended. Because there is nothing in the text that is critical of Sonia, a reader must recognize that Dostoevsky meant her to be the chief exemplar of goodness in the novel. Deciding whether she is believable or likeable is one thing. Discussing how she fits into Dostoevsky's view of the world is another.

Profiry Petrovich

Porfiry represents the authority of the state, or the law, in his pursuit of Raskolnikov. His technique is modeled, in part, on the type of detective that was so popular in 19th-century fiction—an investigator who is able to solve difficult crimes by rational deduction rather than physical investigation.

Although Porfiry does "solve" the case by deducing that Raskolnikov is guilty, his skills as a detective are not of primary interest to Dostoevsky. Rather, the novelist concentrates on the duel of wills between Porfiry and Raskolnikov, two brilliant and egotistical men with very different ideas about what is important in life.

Porfiry is the ony character who is Raskolnikov's intellectual equal, and the only one who understands the complex motives for his crime. The ironic, mocking tone he uses to talk to Raskolnikov reminds some readers of the arrogance Raskolnikov himself shows other people. The investigator's emphasis on psychological analysis as a way of detecting criminals is almost as revolutionary as Raskolnikov's belief in crimes of principle. The major difference between them is that Porfiry's theory stresses the social good, while Raskolnikov's means social anarchy. Some critics suggest that Dostoevsky intends Porfiry to represent Russian solutions to Russian problems in contrast to the Western European sources of Raskolnikov's mistaken theories.

Dostoevsky shows Porfiry opposed to both the legal and the moral transgressions of Raskolnikov's crime. He isn't that interested in putting the criminal behind bars; instead, he's committed to getting Raskolnikov to admit the error of his ways. He embodies Dostoevsky's belief that punishment that is imposed on a criminal does little good if the man himself rejects his own guilt.

Porfiry appears only three times in the novel, but many readers believe he is the second most important character. They argue that without him, Raskolnikov would never have been suspected and, more important, would never have been rehabilitated. Porfiry's success illustrates Dostoevsky's position as a conservative thinker who supports conformity to the law and traditional Christian ethics as the foundations of a productive life.

Porfiry's biggest fans insist that the reason he doesn't appear more often, and simply disappears before the end of the story, is that he's really more interesting and appealing than Raskolnikov. They think that if he were in more of the scenes he would become the novel's hero. There's no way to prove this idea, though. It seems pretty clear that this is Raskolnikov's story.

Arkady Ivanovich Svidrigailov

Because this is Raskolnikov's story, each of the other characters is considered in relation to him. While Svidrigailov's life and death are dramatic in themselves, their importance to the novel lies in what they tell you about Raskolnikov. In literary terms we would say that Svidrigailov (and also Porfiry, Razumikhin, and Luzhin) acts as a foil to Raskolnikov. A foil is a character whose similarities to—and differences from—the main character help to define the main character.

Like Raskolnikov, Svidrigailov is a criminal. He too is troubled by vivid, terrifying dreams: dead characters haunt him, as they do Raskolnikov. The striking moment when the two meet occurs just as Raskolnikov wakes up from reliving in his dream the murder of the pawnbroker. Svidrigailov doesn't waste any time telling him they are "birds of a feather," an idea he repeats frequently.

Like Raskolnikov, he seeks love from a woman who has shown pity for him and who, he believes, will save him from death. In his case the woman he loves—with a great sexual passion—is Raskolnikov's sister Dunya. Unlike Sonia, Dunya spurns her lover's advances. She is repulsed by him, and when he finally understands how much she hates him, he kills himself. In contrast, Raskolnikov's love for Sonia truly is his salvation.

Another similarity between them is that Svidrigailov is generous with his money. Like Raskolnikov, he is the benefactor of the needy, in particular of the Marmeladovs.

Despite the similarities, most readers finally conclude that the differences between the men are more important. For one thing, Svidrigailov is decadent. You might forgive his having been in prison for debt and having allowed a woman to buy his way out. But he is also a child molester, a man who can barely control his passions.

While he argues that he seeks out Dunya as his salvation from evil and boredom, it seems much more likely that he is primarily interested in sexual satisfaction. Many readers are repelled by the fact that he tries to buy her love by threatening to betray her brother as a killer.

It is important to realize, though, that Svidrigailov isn't a totally evil, despicable character. His decision to commit suicide has tragic elements because he's so totally abandoned. He evokes pity from many readers, although they are able to see that he has invited his own destruction. As you read the scenes in which he appears, watch the balance that Dostoevsky strikes between the hateful and the pathetic parts of his character.

As you consider Svidrigailov as a foil to Raskolnikov, ask yourself a few questions: Why does Raskolnikov hate and fear Svidrigailov after his initial, rather favorable, impression? And why is it that Svidrigailov seems to be able to get away with his crimes without all the anguish that Raskolnikov suffers? Does that make Svidrigailov a superman? Remember, though, that in the end Raskolnikov lives and Svidrigailov dies.

Avdotya Romanovna Raskolnikova (Dunya, Dounia)

Raskolnikov's sister may remind you in some ways of Raskolnikov. Dostoevsky stresses how much they look alike and how stubborn and determined they both are. Ultimately, though, Dunya yields to the conventional feminine stereotype and finds happiness in marriage with Razumikhin. That happens, in part, because while she shares her brother's pride and courage to be bold, she lacks his intellectual turmoil. Her rebellion is not as dramatic as his, nor is it criminal.

However, when Svidrigailov threatens her virtue and her brother's safety, she is perfectly willing to kill him and actually tries to. She grazes him with her first shot; the gun misfires the second time. You could argue that it is only lack of skill that keeps her from being a murderer too. She throws down the gun, instead of firing another shot, though. In doing so, she rejects the violence that Raskolnikov tested.

Her potential for violence is like his. But stronger than Dunya's power to hate is her power to love. She loves her brother, her mother, and eventually her husband. Some critics even believe that she feels an attraction for Svidrigailov that is destroyed by his overt sexuality. Like Sonia, she is willing to suffer for those she loves; unlike Sonia, she draws the line.

Like Sonia, too, her love is strong enough to forgive Raskolnikov's transgressions. And Dunya can understand his decision to turn to a prostitute for love and forgiveness. Dunya recognizes his anguish and the struggle it will be for him to recover his mental and emotional balance. Wisely, she also realizes that Sonia is the only one who can help him. Probably Raskolnikov's most foolish error of judgment is not trusting Dunya and her power to forgive.

For many readers Dunya and Razumikhin are the two most normal, appealing characters in the novel. Remember, though, that Dostoevsky is using them as foils to Raskolnikov, rather than as protagonists.

Dmitri Prokofich Razumikhin

You might think that Raskolnikov's friend Razumikhin is all the things Raskolnikov should be. He's poor, but he manages to find enough odd jobs to get by. While he's not as brilliant as Raskolnikov, he's not tortured with theories about his right to commit crime either. On the other hand, he's not as interesting either.

Razumikhin sticks by his friend, even when Raskolnikov's behavior is baffling or rude. It is Razumikhin's respect and admiration that convince many readers that there is more to Raskolnikov than the surly, murdering egotist of the opening chapters. If Svidrigailov shows us the ugly parts of Raskolnikov's character, Razumikhin (whose name is formed from *razum*, which means "reason" or "good sense") shows us the admirable ones.

Because the truth about the murder unfolds slowly for Razumikhin, the reader watches him carefully for a change in attitude, or for rejection of his friend. When his friendship withstands even the recognition of Raskolnikov's guilt, it is a sign that the murderer can be forgiven.

His romance with Dunya is a romantic love story, even in the torturous setting in which it develops. Their interest in each other develops as a result of their mutual concern for Raskolnikov and is encouraged by Raskolnikov's efforts as matchmaker, but their love has a power of its own.

In the midst of all the sordid and ugly relationships depicted in the novel, this one is so strikingly normal and healthy that it proves that human love can flourish and grow even under the most adverse conditions. Dostoevsky seems to take pleasure in this relationship—in its normalcy and in its promise for the future.

Peter Petrovich Luzhin

While there are several examples of criminal behavior in *Crime and Punishment*, there is only character who is repulsive through and through, and that is Luzhin, Dunya's fiancé. While he is guilty only of lying and character defamation—by falsely accusing Sonia of theft—he is portrayed as totally reprehensible.

His chief crime is his overwhelming, relentless arrogance and self-interest. He is the only character who refuses to recognize his own faults. Further, he represents a character type that Dostoevsky despised: the self-satisfied bureaucrat. While he is hardly a central character—he is only in three scenes—he epitomizes Dostoevsky's idea of the worst that man can be.

MINOR CHARACTERS

Alena (Alyona) Ivanovna

She is the pawnbroker whom Raskolnikov kills. Her younger sister *Lizaveta* is also killed. She was a friend of Sonia Marmeladova, and she is described in the novel as meek, gentle, and long-suffering just as Sonia is.

Semen (Semyon) Zakharovich Marmeladov

He is the drunkard who is killed in an accident and who has aroused Raskolnikov's sympathy with the description of the ruin he has brought on his family. His wife's name is *Katerina Ivanovna*. She can't forgive her husband for the misery he has put them through. In the novel she dies of consumption. She has three children from a former marriage: *Polina (Polya, Polenka, Polechka)*; *Lena (Leeda, Lida, Lyona, Lidochka)*; and their brother *Kolya (Kolka)*. The name Marmeladov comes from the root marmelad, which means jam or jelly. It's another example of Dostoevsky's use of psychonyms.

Pulkheria (Pulcheria) Alexandrovna Raskolnikov

She is Rodion and Dunya's mother.

Andrey Semenovich Lebezyatnikov

He is Luzhin's former ward who boards in the same house as the Marmeladovs.

Zosimov (Zossimov)

He is Raskolnikov's doctor.

Alexander Grigorevich Zametov (Zamyotov)

He is the chief police clerk.

Other Elements

SETTING

The setting of *Crime and Punishment* creates an atmosphere in which the dreadful crimes Dostoevsky describes are all too believable. The novel is set in Haymarket Square, a slum section of St. Petersburg notorious for its intolerable living conditions. Because he knew the city so well, and had lived in the kinds of tenement rooms he describes, Dostoevsky is very specific about the sights and smells his characters experience.

By choosing to set the novel in the summer, when the drunken crowds filled the streets and the air reeked, Dostoevsky was able to create the feelings of physical repulsion brought on by an oppressive environment. By mentioning particular street names and tracing the routes of the characters, he was emphasizing the novel's realism. Raskolnikov knows, for instance, that it is exactly 730 steps from his house to the pawnbroker's. Even today, you can walk the route he followed and count the steps. When the physical details are concrete, you tend to accept the rest of the information in the novel too; even the most bizarre things seem believable.

Crime was a very real problem in Russia at the time the novel was written. An especially gruesome ax murder of two old women in Moscow in the summer of 1865 had gotten enormous play in the press, and Dostoevsky clearly had it in mind as he formulated his novel. Drunkenness and prostitution were commonplace, and the gap between the middle class and the poor was enormous. By documenting these facts of life, Dostoevsky provides social history—and even social protest—as part of his study of Raskolnikov's character.

When the scene shifts to Siberia, in the Epilogue, the physical change signals an enormous change in subject matter as well. The transformation of Raskolnikov's character, from arrogant to penitent, happens in the stark, repressive atmosphere of a prison camp. When he is physically confined and publicly humiliated, he is finally able to find meaning in life that he could not discover when he was free to act as he chose.

Because the Epilogue is short, and the emphasis is on Raskolnikov's "resurrection," there isn't much detail about life in prison. Dostoevsky's own prison experience was still vivid in his mind a dozen years after his release, but his purpose in this section is not realism, but resolution of his theme of salvation. That is why Raskolnikov's reconciliation—with Sonia and with his own humanity—takes place at Easter, the Christian season of hope.

THEMES

Here are summaries of the major themes of the novel. Familiarity with Dostoevsky's ideas makes it easier for you to understand what various events mean. It will also help you decide what to concentrate on as you study the novel.

The Criminal As Hero

How would you feel about somebody who killed two women with an ax? Could you think of him sympathetically? Dostoevsky asks you to do just that in *Crime and Punishment*. But he creates a character who is part cold-blooded killer and part compassionate human being. The struggle between those two parts of Raskolnikov's character—his dual personality—is the central theme of the novel.

Dostoevsky explores his character's duality in several ways. He shows his protagonist's wildly contrasting actions and he compares Raskolnikov to vastly different people. Raskolnikov is like the self-sacrificing Dunya in his concern for people who need help, and like the decadent Svidrigailov in his extreme selfishness. He seeks the challenge of Porfiry, to test his intellectual powers, and the love of Sonia, to learn about the possibility of forgiveness. While readers may differ in their feelings about Raskolnikov, they all agree that his experiences are the central focus of the novel.

Human Love and Divine Love

Strangely enough, *Crime and Punishment* is a love story, or rather several love stories. When Raskolnikov is at last able to admit his love for Sonia and respect her enough to accept her beliefs, he begins his journey to salvation. In contrast, when his sister Dunya repels the advances of Svidrigailov, he commits suicide. Dostoevsky suggests that human love is an expression of divine love, with the power to save or damn.

While Raskolnikov's relationship with Sonia is not very romantic, Dostoevsky makes the attraction between Dunya and Razumikhin a more typical love story. Their marriage confirms that love provides hope and joy even when the situation is otherwise bleak. By extension, Dostoevsky suggests that Raskolnikov and Sonia will find a similiar happiness.

What do you think Raskolnikov would have been like if he hadn't found Sonia? Would he have been as sympathetic a character?

The Power of Dreams

Dostoevsky is concerned with probing the world of dreams. Before and after the murder, Raskolnikov has dreams of such startling realism and power that he—and we, too—are not sure if they're dreams or real. Critics interpret the dreams in different ways sometimes; in the dream about the death of the horse (Part I, Chapter 5) various readers think that Raskolnikov resembles the little boy, or the murdering peasant, or the horse, or sometimes all three. But they all agree that Dostoevsky was innovative in using dreams to reveal deep psychological truths about human behavior and to examine the subconscious fears and desires that express themselves in dreams.

Notice, too, that both Svidrigailov and Raskolnikov have frightening dreams at the end of the novel. Both see themselves and their behavior as it really is. The dreams are so persuasive that each man makes a critical decision based on them.

Crime and Its Consequences

Dostoevsky analyzes the effect of criminal behavior, both on the perpetrator and on the people around him. The worst criminals—like Luzhin—think only of personal gain or of revenge. They are doomed to isolation and failure. Others, like Raskolnikov himself, commit more dreadful crimes. But because they can reestablish themselves with their fellow man and with God, they can be salvaged. Dostoevsky does show the effects of environment on the criminal, but he is primarily interested in the internal, not the external, causes of criminal behavior. He believes alienation is the key to both the causes and the consequences of crime.

Raskolnikov believes at first that there are crimes of principle, crimes committed to prove an intellectual point. Because some people are more brilliant or gifted than others, he thinks they have the right to commit crimes to accomplish their goals. What's more, he believes he is one of these extraordinary people.

Dostoevsky rejects the notion that crime can be justified, and he constructs the novel to persuade the reader to reject it, too. He also believes that a character is ultimately responsible for his own behavior and for the consequences of that behavior.

The Power of Suffering

Sonia and Raskolnikov think differently about suffering. She believes suffering makes a person a better human being and that it can be endured because God will reward the sufferer. She can go on living because she believes that all her misery will help her family—and Raskolnikov—and because she believes that God will not let her down.

Raskolnikov insists that suffering is wasted misery. He's impatient with self-sacrifice and intolerant of the notion that God cares. Many readers agree with his view that any good that comes of misery is coincidental, and insufficient to justify so much self-torture.

The structure of the novel proves that Dostoevsky's point of view is like Sonia's: suffering is both necessary and useful. Its efficacy is proved by Raskolnikov's redemption. But readers who find Raskolnikov's repentence unbelievable are not convinced that Dostoevsky is right.

The Effectiveness of Punishment

Can punishment rehabilitate a criminal? Dostoevsky says the answer is yes, under particular circumstances. He insists that when Raskolnikov rec-

ognizes that his alienation from mankind and his egotism are wrong, he is ready to put his crime behind
him and become a new man. The fact that he is in
prison, being punished by the state, seems coincidental to his new awareness of his guilt.

All of the agony he suffers after the murder is as
much a punishment as the prison term. One of his
most painful realizations is that he doesn't measure
up to his own expectations for himself. In the final
analysis his rehabilitation is possible because Sonia's
love and Porfiry's willingness to wait prepare him to
accept Christian ethics as his ruling principle.

The rest of the criminals and evil-doers aren't so
lucky. Because they are unloved, they are doomed,
according to Dostoevsky, and can't be rehabilitated.
Can you think of some other reasons why Luzlin and
Svidrigailov don't seem to change?

Is There an Objective Morality?

Dostoevsky makes very clear that he believes that
man must live by an objective ethical standard.
Things are either right or they are wrong. Ethics are
not relative. According to this interpretation, Raskolnikov had no right to murder the old lady, no matter
what his reasons. The novelist rejects the idea of a
murder of principle.

Yet, at the same time, he suggests that immoral and
even illegal behavior can be forgiven. Sonia's prostitution doesn't keep her from God; Dunya's lies to shield
her mother from Raskolnikov's trial are justifiable.
Even Raskolnikov is a better person after he tests himself and admits his failure and guilt. In other words,
some standards of morality are more objective than
others. For Dostoevsky, the unforgivable sins are an
overwhelming sense of self-importance and sexual
depravity.

A Detective Story

Crime and Punishment is an unconventional mystery. The crime itself is solved. In fact, you know from the beginning who is guilty. The unanswered question is what Raskolnikov's motive in killing the pawnbroker really was. He offers several reasons, but he rejects them himself, even before the reader gets a chance. The ones that seem the most logical—that he needed the money and that he was testing himself to see if he was extraordinary—are contradictory.

The detective story is unusual too because both the killer and the detective are sympathetic characters. Intellectually they are well matched, but Porfiry has the upper hand in their duels of wit because he is right and Raskolnikov is wrong. Porfiry doesn't follow the usual physical clues either, but observes Raskolnikov's behavior, which he can't keep himself from revealing. The suspense is psychological, and the detective's major aim is Raskolnikov's redemption, not his arrest.

The Power of Fate

Fate means different things in *Crime and Punishment*. Raskolnikov says over and over that Fate caused his actions. For instance, when he overhears that the pawnbroker will be alone, he says Fate ordains that he will kill her. Dostoevsky rejects, and wants the reader to reject, this notion of Fate as the power that predetermines events. The novel makes very clear that Raskolnikov chooses to act, despite his own eagerness to blame Fate.

But Fate also means the doom or ruin of a character as the consequence of his actions and behavior. In this way Fate does play a part in Raskolnikov's story, at least until the miraculous change in the Epilogue. He determines his own destruction by the things that he does; in other words, his Fate is to commit crime because of his arrogance, and to be punished for that crime.

Fate as the inevitable consequence of man's actions is a recurrent theme in the great classical tragedies, and many readers think that Raskolnikov resembles the tragic heroes, whose personalities doom them to disaster.

STYLE

Unless you're fluent in Russian and are reading the novel in its original language, your impression of Dostoevsky's style will be influenced by the translation you read as well as by the novelist's choice of words and sentence structure. The translator's own style makes a big difference.

For instance, the last sentences of Part One read like this in one translation:

> He did not sleep, but lay there in a stupor. If anybody had entered the room he would have sprung up at once with a cry. Disjointed scraps and fragments of ideas floated through his mind, but he could not seize one of them, or dwell upon any, in spite of all his efforts . . . .

In another, the same sentences read like this:

> He did not fall asleep, but lay there in a sort of stupor. If anyone had come into the room, he would at once have leapt screaming to his feet. Scraps and fragments of thoughts swarmed in his head; but he could not fix his mind on a single one of them, he could not concentrate on a single one of them even for a short time, much as he tried to . . . .

A third version says:

> He did not sleep, but sank into blank forgetfulness. If anyone had come into his room then, he would have jumped up and screamed. Scraps and

> shreds of thoughts were simply swarming in his brain, but he could not catch at one, he could not rest on one, in spite of all his efforts . . . .

Perhaps the chief difference between reading Dostoevsky in the original and reading him in translation is that the subtlety of the language is sometimes unavoidably lost. When Dostoevsky calls his protagonist Raskolnikov, he uses the name because the Russian word *raskol* means split or schism; the name helps define the character. Naming characters in this way is a frequent literary device, but it works only when the reader recognizes the connection.

Similarly, the Russian word for crime, *prestuplenie*, is literally translated as a stepping across or a transgression. The physical image of crime as a crossing over of a barrier or a boundary is lost in translation. So is the religious implication of transgression, which we use in English to refer to a sin rather than a crime. Dostoevsky wants you to think of Raskolnikov's action as both.

There are other things, though, that translation doesn't affect. Dostoevsky uses different speech mannerisms and sentences of differing lengths for different characters. Those who use artificial language when they speak—Luzhin, for example, sounds like a pompous businessman, while Lebeziatnikov's speech resembles that of a half-baked politician—are identified as unattractive people. Mrs. Marmeladov's disintegrating mind is reflected in her language too. You can learn a lot about individual characters not only by what they say but how they say it.

POINT OF VIEW

Raskolnikov's story is told by an omniscient narrator, a nameless voice that reports to the reader everything that the characters do and say and also what they think. Most of the time the narrator keeps his opinions to himself, simply revealing the thoughts and actions of Raskolnikov and the others.

There's a lot of dialogue (when two or more characters talk together) and interior monologue (when a character's thoughts are expressed as if they were spoken). The narrator makes no comment about these ideas either. But he does describe the physical environment, the looks on people's faces, and the levels of tension between them. Most of the time what you learn is what Raskolnikov sees or feels; that's a clue that he is the central focus of the novel.

Since Raskolnikov is the major character, almost everything the narrator tells the reader is about him too. The other characters and events are described primarily for what they reveal about Raskolnikov. There are, for instance, only a few scenes in which he doesn't appear; and at those times he remains the focus of attention, even when he's not physically present. For instance, we see the conniving Luzhin and the decadent Svidrigailov away from Raskolnikov, but only when they're doing things that make Raskolnikov seem like a basically decent person in comparison.

Similarly, the narrator shows you the warm affection Raskolnikov's family and friends feel for him in a few scenes where he isn't present. These scenes help you realize that Raskolnikov has many good qualities that can't be ignored when you decide what he's really like. So while it's true that the narrator doesn't say "Hate this character," or "Love this one," the details you're given lead you to the conclusions that Dostoevsky intends.

An omniscient (or all-knowing) narrator is a favorite device of authors writing complicated novels, because it is an effective method for giving the reader a comprehensive view of several characters. Dostoevsky worked with several other approaches before he finished planning *Crime and Punishment*. He considered a first-person narration, with Raskolnikov telling his own story, and a combination of first-person and third-person narrators. His final choice was a narrator who could see the events from many perspectives and let you do the same.

Just as the protagonist of the novel isn't an exact autobiographical image of the author, neither is the narrator. His point of view isn't *exactly* the same as the author's. The narrator is as much a creation as any of the characters is; you have to decide if he's someone you can believe, just as you have to decide when Raskolnikov is being honest. Most readers, however, find this narrator a clear and honest filter through whom they can grasp Dostoevsky's ideas.

FORM AND STRUCTURE

Crime and Punishment has a distinct beginning, middle, and end. Its structure helps to reinforce the title and some of the major themes of the novel. Part One describes the crime. Parts Two through Six explore the physical and emotional consequences of that crime on the killer (his punishment). The seventh part of the novel, the Epilogue, presents the resolution of his case.

A gruesome ax murder is the climax of Part One. Because Dostoevsky isn't concerned primarily with the causes of crime, the events that lead to the murder move quickly and take up only three days. This section also introduces, by name, all but one of the major characters. By the time the pawnbroker dies, everything is in place to bring her killer to justice.

The five central sections of the novel recount the events that force Raskolnikov to confess. When he planned his crime, he was alone—isolated; afterwards he is forced into the company of others. Because he must react to them, he is forced to behave differently and to think differently too.

The last part, the Epilogue is set apart from the rest both in time and place. Raskolnikov is in prison in Siberia. Eighteen months have passed since the crime. At the conclusion of the section he is renewed, reborn, and looks forward to the end of his sentence with hope of a new life.

The number 7 is often considered a "magic" number, with special religious meaning. According to the Bible, for example, God created the world in six days and rested on the seventh. Many readers believe that Dostoevsky deliberately structured his novel in seven parts to make his message about Raskolnikov's new beliefs stronger. Even readers who find the change in Raskolnikov hard to believe have to admit that the structure seems to prove Dostoevsky planned his conclusion carefully and didn't just tack it on at the end.

The Story

PART I

CHAPTER 1

From the moment you begin reading about Raskolnikov holed up in his filthy attic room, you know he's a complicated person. He's paralyzed with dread as he plans a mysterious "terrible act." Although he doesn't say what the act is, he calls it "horrible" and "repulsive"; you get the feeling it must be a crime. But as awful as his plan apparently is, what he seems most afraid of is that he won't be able to go through with it. You can sense from these contradictory feelings that Raskolnikov is in mental and emotional turmoil. He worries about everything, and he's cut himself off from everybody. That's a pretty reliable clue to his state of mind.

To show that Raskolnikov is the central character in the novel, and that what he does and thinks are its subject, Dostoevsky introduces several mysteries about him in this chapter. Some of them get solved as the novel develops. But often the clues seem contradictory or lead you in several directions at once. This is one way Dostoevsky keeps you reading—by raising provocative questions you want answered.

By describing the poverty and ugliness of the environment, Dostoevsky explains some of Raskolnikov's behavior and makes you understand how a sensitive person might act strangely, even abnormally, under such conditions. When he leaves his garret, he's revolted by the hot, smelly streets and the drunken people. He's lightheaded because he hasn't eaten for two days, and he owes lots of money.

The only way to get cash is from a pawnbroker. But when he tries to pawn his father's watch, you can see how pathetic his situation is. It tears him apart to pawn something of such great sentimental value, but in the pawnbroker's eyes, the watch is practically worthless. She shows no sympathy. "Take it or leave it" is the way she does business. Raskolnikov takes the money. But the mystery grows about the "terrible act" he's been planning. He calls the visit to the pawnbroker a "rehearsal," although he doesn't say what he's rehearsing.

Dostoevsky teases the reader and breaks the tension by having Raskolnikov enter a tavern, suddenly wanting to be friendly. Raskolnikov himself is aware that his rapid changes of mood are strange, even weird. It's hard to say which is more perplexing: his behavior or the plan he hints at but doesn't explain. All you can tell for sure is that he agonizes about himself constantly.

CHAPTER 2

The solitary drinker who fascinates Raskolnikov at the end of the first chapter dominates Chapter 2 with his tortured confession. Unlike the morose, brooding Raskolnikov, the drunken Marmeladov is talkative and seems almost to enjoy describing his misery and self-hatred. He recounts every bitter detail of the ruin he has brought on his family. The most pathetic is the miserable story about his daughter, who has been driven to prostitution by the family's poverty.

Marmeladov calls Sonia meek, a word with Christian overtones, and describes her as a fragile wisp of a person without education or skills. He has failed her as a father, and her stepmother has taunted her into providing money for the starving family with her only asset: her body. Sonia's prostitution is a social com-

mentary on the breakdown of traditional family structure and emphasizes the desperate plight of poor
women.

But Sonia is also eternally forgiving, according to
her father. She gives her family money when she has
nothing for herself; Marmeladov calls her a saint who
will be forgiven by God for her sins. That hope keeps
him alive.

NOTE: It is ironic that Marmeladov, a degenerate
drunk, introduces the religious ideas that are so
important to the rest of the novel. He believes in forgiveness, mercy, and the power of suffering—ideas
that, at first, are totally alien to Raskolnikov's way of
thinking. Repeatedly, the older man insists that
everybody needs somewhere or someone to turn to.
Without that refuge, he says, a person is doomed.
Marmeladov believes that even he will be forgiven,
although you may not be convinced he should be.
Dostoevsky never lets on what he himself really
thinks about Marmeladov, so you have to decide for
yourself.

When Raskolnikov escorts the drunkard home, the
young man is appalled at the squalor in which the
family lives and the evidence of the consumption (tuberculosis) that is killing Marmeladov's wife Katerina
Ivanovna. Dostoevsky also shows us the violence that
poverty can bring. Katerina Ivanovna abuses her children, and she assaults her husband when he returns
penniless, jobless, and drunk.

Impulsively, Raskolnikov leaves them money on
the windowsill, but he hates himself for being so soft.
Dostoevsky is showing us a new side of his character,
an ability to feel sorry for people worse off than he
is.

Though he speaks of Sonia ironically as their gold mine, you can find evidence of his capacity for compassion when he thinks about how her family takes her money: "They wept at first, but now they are used to it. Men are scoundrels; they can get used to anything!"

NOTE: We learn in this chapter of the 30 silver roubles Sonia earned on her first night as a prostitute. This is a clear reference to the thirty pieces of silver that Judas got for betraying Christ. References to betrayal, death, and resurrection occur frequently in the novel and are directly linked to the theme that suffering is rewarded. The allusion to the Christ story works, even though Sonia—unlike Judas—is the betrayed, not the betrayer. You might even say she's the one who is Christ-like.

This chapter is important because it shows a new side of Raskolnikov's character, and because he hears about Sonia. You'll see later why that matters.

CHAPTER 3

The picture of poverty that has already been introduced in the first two chapters is expanded even more in the description of Raskolnikov's room and his desperate existence.

NOTE: The dusty, shredding wallpaper in Raskolnikov's garret is yellow, a color Dostoevsky uses repeatedly in the novel to suggest decay, degeneracy, and corruption. The pawnbroker's fur jacket is yellow with age; the identity card Sonia carries as a prostitute is yellow. Near the end of the novel, when Svidrigailov has the dream that drives him to suicide, the wallpaper in the room is yellow, too (Part VI, Chapter 6). As you read the novel, watch for other examples of this color symbolism.

Raskolnikov's feelings about his family are the most important things we discover in this chapter, as he reads a long awaited letter from his mother. It is strange to think of Raskolnikov as a loving son after the ways he has behaved up until this point in the novel, but his affection for his mother and sister is critical to any sympathetic understanding of him. Many readers think it's the most normal thing about him.

The letter reveals that his mother and sister have had a dreadful two months, too, during the time he's been so isolated. And their problems become his problems, including Dunya's difficulties with the lecherous Svidrigailov, her former employer. Because the letter arrives when it does, the news of his sister Dunya's engagement to the civil servant Luzhin becomes a critical factor in Raskolnikov's final decision to carry out his terrible plan. Or, at least, it's a good excuse.

For much of the chapter, Raskolnikov is passive, as he was in Chapter 2. As he reads the letter, there is at first no evidence of his reaction. What Dostoevsky asks us to do is form our own opinion of what Pulkheria Raskolnikova is telling her son. You hear two things: (1) the essentially factual account of Svidrigailov's attempts to seduce Dunya while she was his children's governess; and (2) the more ambiguous account of Dunya's engagement.

Raskolnikov's mother repeats several of her points for emphasis. Dunya is an angel who loves her brother. Luzhin has some unpleasant qualities, but he is very successful. And the marriage is going to guaran-

tee Raskolnikov's future. She tells him that, because
her credit has improved on the strength of the proposed marriage, she will be able to send him thirty
roubles to tide him over, especially if she economizes
and travels third class to St. Petersburg for Dunya's
wedding. Thirty roubles is so clear a reminder of Sonia's earnings as a prostitute that the suggestion of
Dunya selling herself for her family is inescapable.

Raskolnikov is so furious when he finishes the letter
that he must escape from his room; his anger should
confirm your uneasy sense that something about the
proposed marriage is very wrong. But notice again
that Dostoevsky doesn't tell you what to think.

CHAPTER 4

Raskolnikov once more assumes center stage in this
chapter, as he expresses his outrage at his sister's
approaching marriage. Again, watch what he does
and listen to what he says for clues to his complex
character. His ability to read between the lines of his
mother's evasive letter and his refusal to allow Dunya
to sacrifice herself for him seem to many readers
assertive signs of his intelligence and humanity.

The letter has arrived at a critical moment. Raskolnikov, fresh from his evening with Marmeladov,
focuses on the parallels he sees between his own family and the drunkard's. He decides that he, like Marmeladov, is the unworthy recipient of someone else's
sacrifice and self-denial. In his mind, Dunya is selling
herself exactly as Sonia has done. In fact, he decides
that Dunya is more corrupt because she is selling herself for luxuries, while Sonia is acting out of despera-
tion, to ensure her family's survival. How can Raskolnikov prevent the sacrifice and the marriage? How
can he avoid being more indebted to his sister?

Inevitably, he returns to the mysterious, horrible plan of the opening chapter. He must act to stop the marriage, or else he must give up and submit. But the action he plans is still buried in his anguished consciousness. The reader is still uncertain what it will mean. Does his decision to act suggest a devoted brother acting to rescue his sister from an unhappy life? Or is this a handy, irrational excuse to do what he wants?

CHAPTER 5

Rather than answer the questions raised at the end of Chapter 4, Dostoevsky adds further complications as the pace of Raskolnikov's struggle speeds up.

Having tried to work out his confused feelings on a long walk, Raskolnikov falls asleep and dreams a horrible dream, the first of many that will plague him.

NOTE: Dreams play a major role in the novel. They are closely tied to important events, especially violent ones. Dostoevsky was one of the first novelists to use dreams to show the mental and emotional turmoil of characters. This is one of the ways that he anticipates and even influences modern ideas about human behavior, particularly the psychological interpretation of dreams.

Raskolnikov in particular has many different kinds of dreams that show you the ideas and emotions warring in his mind. Some of his dreams reveal or predict the future; others recreate the terrors of the past. His first and most dramatic nightmare does both.

Raskolnikov dreams that he is once again a child, reunited with his long-dead father. As they walk through their rural village, the boy stares in horror as an aged horse is beaten to death by her drunken master. He must watch; it is a compulsion, though others try to lead him away. He hysterically embraces the dead animal's bloody head and tries to assault the violent peasant who has killed the mare.

He awakes in a cold sweat, confused and almost irrational. For the first time he speaks his horrible plan: to smash the pawnbroker's head with an ax and steal her money. His violent tendencies have been revealed in his dream. But so have his fear and revulsion of violence, which make him identify not only with the killer, but with the little boy who is appalled at the scene, and even with the horse who is the victim.

You may feel an enormous sense of relief as Raskolnikov comes to terms with his dream. He resolves not to commit the crime. He even prays that God will show him how to escape his evil thoughts. But does he give up his plan because he believes it is wrong or because he lacks the courage to go through with it? Readers have seen both of these possibilities in his decision.

Moments later his resolve, his humanity, is ambushed. Fate, he insists, changes his life. For he overhears that the pawnbroker's meek and mild sister, Lizaveta, will be away from home at seven the next evening. All questions, all struggles evaporate: his victim will be home alone.

He calls it fate, but is it really a convenient excuse?

CHAPTER 6

The debate about fate continues as Raskolnikov retraces the growth of his plan. Has fate really played a part in directing the murder? Does chance have that much influence on human behavior? Raskolnikov insists it does, even long after the crime has been committed. You may wonder. Dostoevsky doesn't say directly what he thinks, but he does give you some clues that Raskolnikov makes the decisions that he wants to make. Events and emotions may help explain why he acts, but the decisions are *his*.

We learn that he has known about the pawnbroker for six months, and that he first visited her six weeks before the novel begins. We don't find out here, or ever, what made him give up his jobs and his communication with others about that time. He explains, though, that he began to feel superstitious and to believe that coincidence was helping to further his own evil plans and ideas.

The revulsion that he felt for the old lady the first time he saw her is also intimately connected with his plan to kill her. He was not alone in his hatred of her. The very night he met her, he overheard her described as a selfish and abusive louse who plans to leave all the money she has extorted from poor people to a monastery. There the money will buy perpetual prayers for the repose of her soul.

The student who described Alena Ivanovna as a louse and detailed the way she mistreats her long-suffering sister also insisted that it would be doing humanity a favor to murder the old hag:

> Kill her, take her money, on condition that you dedicate yourself with its help to the service of humanity and the common good: don't you think that thousands of good deeds will wipe out one little, insignificant transgression?

The idea couldn't have found a more receptive audience—or one more likely to act—than the eavesdropping Raskolnikov. How closely the student's ideas support his own! The conversation seemed to him a profound coincidence, "as if there were indeed something fateful and fore-ordained about it." But is he really killing to serve humanity—or simply to prove something to himself? Readers have argued that question ever since the novel was published.

The day of the murder, the third day of the story, Raskolnikov sleeps most of the time. He has worked out many details of the murder plan already. His careful planning makes his crime seem more appalling, more evil—to himself and to us. For many people, it is easier to forgive an impetuous, spur-of-the-moment murder than one which is premeditated (planned). Our laws distinguish clearly between premeditated and accidental murder.

NOTE: Raskolnikov spends a lot of time thinking about crime and criminals. He has a theory that criminals become physically and mentally ill when they commit crimes. They are unable to use their reason when they need it most, to avoid detection. One question he can't answer is whether the illness causes crime, or the crime causes illness. It is a question that people are still asking about mental competence and criminal behavior, especially in cases that use insanity defenses. As you read the novel, think about where you stand on this issue.

Raskolnikov insists at one point that, unlike a common criminal, he won't get sick or be unable to function at the time of the murder, because what he is planning is "no crime." This idea may take you by surprise, and the idea is dropped as suddenly as it was raised. Later on, though, it will turn out to be very important in understanding his motives for killing.

Raskolnikov's erratic behavior quickens as the fatal hour approaches. Time slips away; he is late; he must find an axe; he curses his distinctive hat. Despite some holes in his plan and some careless mistakes, "luck" or fate seems to push Raskolnikov closer and closer to the "terrible act" that's been obsessing him. At last he reaches the pawnbroker's door. It is his third, fatal visit, and he rings the doorbell three ominous times.

NOTE: The number 3 is sometimes used as a signal of doom. One modern usage you might compare is "Three strikes and you're out." Dostoevsky uses the number 3 over and over. Watch for it. It's almost always a signal.

CHAPTER 7

The tension explodes in the murder of the pawnbroker. Raskolnikov hits her on top of her head three times with the blunt end of an axe. She dies instantly.

Does Raskolnikov react as he theorized he would? Do his will and reason, which he needs to get away with his crime, hold up? Why does he shake so much that he can barely remove the keys from the pawnbroker's body? He is terrified that he is losing his mind.

At first taking care not to get bloody, but finally smearing his hand in the blood, he snatches the dead woman's purse from its hiding place around her neck. Then he uses her keys to unlock her trunk. But he has only begun to stuff his pockets with gold "pledges" when a faint sound from the other room startles him.

Momentarily, he crouches, unable to breathe, and then he bursts into the murder room, axe clutched in his hand. Lizaveta, the pawnbroker's sister, has returned. Stunned, she stares in horror and backs away, one hand feebly trying to ward off the blow she knows will come. Everything has gone wrong.

Using one swift blow with the blade of the axe, Raskolnikov splits open the head of the horrified woman. Terror washes over him. The unpremeditated murder affects him as the execution of the old woman had not. Reason deserts him. Deliberately, slowly, he washes his hands and the axe and examines everything for stains. Minutes tick by, but he makes no effort to flee until suddenly the urgency to get away strikes him like a bolt.

Again the tension builds. The front door is open. Someone might have seen! He slams it closed and bolts it, locking himself in with his victims. Then momentary calm returns, and he once again prepares to leave—only to be confronted with footsteps mounting the stairs. Instinctively, he knows they are coming to the pawnbroker's.

Locking the door quietly, strangely calm, Raskolnikov waits inside while first one man and then two ring the bell and rattle the door handle. How can the inevitable be avoided? His capture is surely just a matter of minutes away.

But the ironic luck which has been with him all along rescues him again. The confused men leave in search of the porter to find out what is going on. Raskolnikov slips away, hiding briefly in an empty apartment and finally returning to his own room, carefully replacing the axe where he found it.

Two women are dead. Their killer has gotten away, apparently unnoticed, leaving no clues behind. He has proved his theory: if you keep your will and your

reason, you can get away with murder. Or has he? He
flings himself onto the sofa in his room and falls into a
stupor.

PART II

CHAPTER 1

Hours later, still in a stupor and once again isolated
in his garret, Raskolnikov tries to cope with the memory of the murders. Chills and tremors plague him,
and he compulsively examines his clothes for blood-
stains. Suddenly he remembers the loot in his coat
pockets and hides it behind the torn wallpaper without counting the money. One thing the murders
haven't changed is the self-doubt that haunts him.

Rushing around the room, he seems unable to
decide what to do next. He cuts off the bloody fringes
of his trousers and tears the stained pocket from his
coat, but can't figure out what to do with them. "Can
this really be the beginning of my punishment?" he
asks. Punishment is something that he has never
thought about until now. By showing Raskolnikov's
hysteria, Dostoevsky picks up on one of the young
man's theories—that illness accompanies crime. Does
his reaction prove that he has committed a crime after
all? Remember, he was sure he wouldn't react the
way an ordinary criminal would.

His only solution is to go to sleep. But he awakes to
a loud knocking on the door. His first thought is that
he has been found out. In his state he doesn't realize
how unlikely that is; he debates with himself about
how he should respond. Finally, he simply opens the
door. His worst imaginings seem confirmed when he
is handed a summons from the police. Once more,
Dostoevsky draws the reader into Raskolnikov's anx-
iety. Is it all over already?

In fact, the summons is absolutely unrelated to the murder. But Raskolnikov can't pull himself together. Fear that he will give himself away tortures him. He is in such a state that he leaves his room unlocked, with the bloody shreds of clothing lying in plain sight and the pawnbroker's money and possessions clumsily hidden. The coincidental summons (foreshadowed by the maid in Part I, Chapter 3) and the tension it produces are Dostoevsky's way of showing us Raskolnikov's fragile grip on himself. No wonder Raskolnikov's worried about giving himself away. He ought to be.

His inner confusion is profound when he arrives at the station and confronts, in turn, three representatives of the police: Zametov, the chief-clerk; Ilya Petrovich, the fiery lieutenant; and Nikodim Fomich, the captain. When he learns from the clerk that he is being sued for his debts, relief washes over him. Enough of his old arrogance returns so that he can even talk back to the lieutenant. You may be able to remember reacting this way yourself, when you've gotten away with a close call. For all his strangeness, Raskolnikov is a very real character.

In his euphoria, he tells the sad story of his crushing debt and his unhappy life, but the officers aren't impressed. Clearly there is nothing new in his experience, and they're callous about suffering. Their lack of interest depresses Raskolnikov profoundly, another indication of his emotional state, for "his soul . . . was tormentingly conscious of . . . eternal loneliness and estrangement." His alienation from his fellow men is increasing.

He feels an urge to confess, to get it over with, to tell all. But he resists just in time to overhear the three men engrossed in a conversation about the pawnbroker's mysterious murder. Then, when he stands up to leave, he faints. A more dramatic moment is hard to imagine.

Suddenly, everybody is enormously interested in him. But now their interest fills Raskolnikov with fear and dread.

CHAPTER 2

To get rid of the incriminating purse and trinkets, Raskolnikov gathers them up and decides to throw them all into the canal. He still hasn't counted the money, and he never does. While he was planning the murder, Raskolnikov had claimed he wanted the old woman's money so that he could help others—especially his sister. This motivation doesn't occur to him now, in his fearful state.

Rejecting the canal because people might see him, Raskolnikov walks on toward the Neva River. But before he gets there, he changes his mind and buries the loot in a deserted lot, under a stone behind an open drainage ditch. None of this behavior suggests a man of will and reason.

The more he thinks about his behavior with the police, the more he blames himself for cringing and being afraid. Worse, he hates himself for not counting the money. The only excuse he can find is that he is ill, a recognition that fills him with hatred for everyone, including himself. After all, before the murder wasn't he sure he was different from everybody else?

For a reason he can't really explain, he reaches out for companionship and goes to visit his old friend Razumikhin whom he hasn't seen for four months. One interpretation of this decision is that there is a hidden part of him that wants to put his actions behind him. By seeking out his old friends, he can start over. Perhaps it is more honest to recognize that

Raskolnikov is physically ill—something his friend realizes almost immediately—and simply needs help.

In his delirium, Raskolnikov struggles to explain why he has come and why he can't stay, why he doesn't want work although he is desperate for money. Even the generous Razumikhin is angry at his baffling behavior. Clearly, Raskolnikov doesn't know what he wants.

Still ill, he wanders into the street, where he is nearly run down by a team of horses. The shock, and a small amount of money a compassionate passerby hands him, bring him back to his senses for a moment. But what he realizes about himself disturbs him. His past is gone because of his crime; he is cut off from it.

By nightfall, he is seriously ill. He hallucinates that his landlady is being beaten by the police lieutenant, and he's so exhausted from listening to the imaginary incident that he falls unconscious.

This chapter reestablishes Raskolnikov's link with his old friend and his former life. Now all of the primary characters have been introduced, and Dostoevsky can begin to develop Raskolnikov by showing him in relation to other people.

CHAPTER 3

The physical and emotional collapse that Raskolnikov suffers in the next few days—a nervous breakdown we would call it today—makes him totally dependent on others. The chief architect of his recovery is Razumikhin, the person to whom he had turned in his wretched reaction to the murders.

Razumikhin has taken charge: it is a role he will maintain for Raskolnikov's family for the rest of the story. He has brought a doctor, cajoled the landlady, and got necessary information from the police to retrieve the damaging IOU. With the money Raskolnikov's mother sends, he buys the young man an entirely new wardrobe.

As Raskolnikov begins to realize how many people have been around and how sick he's been, he grows desperate to know if, in his delirium, he has revealed his guilty secret. He may be part of society again as far as other people are concerned, but still considers himself separate. And he knows how important it is to keep his secret. This tension even keeps him from enjoying Razumikhin's rather infectious humor. He longs to be alone, even to run away to America (a place Dostoevsky uses frequently in his fiction as a goal for all sorts of disreputable people!).

CHAPTER 4

Although Raskolnikov takes no part in the conversations in this chapter—one about Razumikhin's plans for a housewarming party that evening and another about the murder of the pawnbroker—he is keenly interested in the second conversation, and obviously directly involved. But he is the only one who knows it.

Because Razumikhin has invited the police clerk Zametov and the examining magistrate, Porfiry Petrovich, to his party, the talk quickly turns to the murder. Razumikhin explains he disapproves of the way the investigation is being handled. One of the painters who had been working in the pawnbroker's building on the evening of the killing has been arrested, but Razumikhin and his friends are sure he's innocent.

In the middle of the discussion, one remark unsettles Raskolnikov completely, and he spends the rest of the time staring at the wall. The maid announces, quite out of the blue, that the murdered Lizaveta had once mended one of his shirts. This is another of the coincidences that fill the novel. Readers disagree on whether details like this make the novel more realistic and powerful, or too artificial and contrived. It's something you might think about.

Besides providing details of what the police know about the murder—which isn't much—the conversation provides some serious criticism of police methods of investigation. Razumikhin accuses them of arresting first and thinking afterward, and of not asking the right questions. The strongest criticism, and the one that has the most bearing on Raskolnikov, is the one that bothers Razumikhin the most: the investigators will interpret even the least significant physical evidence as important while ignoring psychological evidence about the accused's mental state. With opposition like that, Raskolnikov has little to fear, and he knows it.

CHAPTER 5

The stranger who comes to the door in the middle of this conversation about the murder is looking for Raskolnikov. But his identity is a shock. He's Peter Petrovich Luzhin, Dunya's fiancé, the man Raskolnikov is prepared to despise. Very little time passes before all Raskolnikov's fears about him are justified. Luzhin is pompous and patronizing, egotistical and ignorant. In response, Raskolnikov and Razumikhin are rude.

Luzhin's expensive and ostentatious wardrobe is described in detail, and so are the cheap hotel rooms he has rented for Dunya and her mother. His character is further defined when he tries to ingratiate himself with the young people by espousing views that he

thinks they wish to hear, but which really express his
own view of life. His ideas are that (1) people should
love themselves first, and (2) that what is good, eco-
nomically, for the individual will ultimately help others.

NOTE: The selfishness and essential immorality
of Luzhin's ideas are at the heart of what Dostoevsky
defines as crime in the novel. Notice how frequently
this crime of "me first" comes up.

Ignoring his presence, Razumikhin and Zosimov
return to their discussion of the murderer. He must,
they think, have been a client of the pawnbroker.
Suddenly, Raskolnikov rouses from his lethargy. Cli-
ents being interrogated! That demands his full attention.

Unwittingly, Razumikhin tortures his friend by
describing what he thinks the murderer must be like:
an inexperienced criminal saved by chance from being
discovered at his first attempt at crime. Chance, or fate
(which Raskolnikov has already identified as a powerful force in his life) is now suggested as the most
important element in the murderer's success. The
criminal's inexperience is proved, Razumikhin insists,
by the fact that he left 1500 roubles untouched in the
dresser drawer. Perhaps the most perceptive thing he
says is that the killer must have lost his head. Hearing
that doesn't help Raskolnikov's self-respect.

Luzhin tries to get back into the conversation by
asking—rhetorically—why there is so much crime.
Razumikhin suggests that crime is easier than work,
but it is Raskolnikov who has the more provocative

answer. If people believe that they should serve themselves first, that is adequate explanation for crime. People like Luzhin who advocate such ideas are to blame.

Raskolnikov presses his point even further. The fact that Luzhin prefers a poor wife who will have to be grateful to him is also criminal. Suddenly, the accusation is very personal. Whatever chance the two might have had for tolerating each other has dissolved. Luzhin criticizes Raskolnikov's mother. Raskolnikov, in turn, threatens assault.

The furious Luzhin leaves, and Raskolnikov insists that the others leave too. But his irrationality amazes his friend and his doctor, and they resolve to figure out what is on his mind. Both are fascinated by his passionate interest in the murder; his determination to be alone has found determined enemies.

CHAPTER 6

After several chapters (and days) of being passive, Raskolnikov reasserts himself. Still weak and dizzy, he feels he must leave his repulsive room. When he is alone and calm again, he dresses in his new clothes, pockets the remaining twenty-five roubles from his mother, and leaves his room.

Nothing has changed in the city, although he has felt an enormous transformation in himself since the murders. He is desperate to resolve the conflicting feelings that plague him. He feels he can no longer live an unresolved life. But he has no idea how to go about changing things and cannot bear to think about it. You might decide he really hasn't changed very much, despite what he thinks.

The beggars, drunks, and prostitutes he passes in the street depress him, but he grasps at one insight: that people prefer to live under the most dreadful circumstances rather than to die. This thought recurs to him many times in the days that follow; you might say it's what keeps him alive.

Entering a tavern in order to find the newspaper accounts of the murder, Raskolnikov finds himself—again by coincidence—with Zametov, the police clerk. Far from trying to disguise his fascination with the murder story, Raskolnikov flaunts his interest in it. What seems even more self-destructive is that he taunts Zametov until the clerk says what is on the reader's mind: "Either you are mad, or. . . ."

How else can you explain what Raskolnikov is doing? He uses words like confess and reminds Zametov that he fainted when the murder was discussed in the police station. Many critics have suggested he does this because he wants to be caught. They think he is unable to deal with his own sense of guilt and uncertainty. Others think that he is testing himself and tormenting Zametov for his own amusement. Either way, this is a critical conversation. You will discover later that Raskolnikov's behavior in the tavern is one of the reasons Porfiry Petrovich is so sure he's the killer.

Crime is the topic of conversation. What better subject for a police clerk and a killer? At last Raskolnikov has an opportunity to express his ideas on how crimes can be committed effectively. And it gives Zametov a chance to talk about the mistakes that were made at the murder of the pawnbroker. Again, Raskolnikov seems to be taking crazy risks, as he explains what he would have done: bury the money he had stolen.

Pushing even further, he asks, "What if it was I who killed the old woman and Lizaveta?" It is hard to tell which of them is more upset by the conversation; Raskolnikov seems the less flustered. For some readers his behavior is evidence that he's mentally unbalanced—mad, as Zametov would say.

NOTE: You can't be sure what Zametov is thinking during his conversation with Raskolnikov. Because the reader knows the identity of the murderer from the start, it is hard to tell how much either Zametov or Razumikhin has figured out at any given time. That's one of the ways Dostoevsky builds suspense.

Leaving the tavern, Raskolnikov runs into Razumikhin. His friend is genuinely, deeply concerned about him, but Raskolnikov responds by being incredibly rude. He insists he is sane, responsible, and unwilling to bother with other people. By the time he finishes with his attack, he is furiously angry, "raving madly and choking with rage."

Razumikhin's anger at this treatment is justified. The fact that he will not allow himself to be abused affirms him as a strong and appealing character. But because he is a good friend, his anger dissolves into concern. He encourages Raskolnikov to forget the unpleasantness between them and come to his party.

Refusing, Raskolnikov leaves. After a fruitless attempt to follow him, Razumikhin goes back to Zametov to find out what has happened. Don't underestimate the importance of Razumikhin's affection for Raskolnikov. One of the things that contributes to our feeling that Raskolnikov has good qualities despite his actions is that people whom we admire love him. In a complex novel, the reaction of others to a character is critical to your ability to make a judgment yourself.

As Raskolnikov walks on, he gets weaker and weaker. He feels that he is about to faint again, when he is startled by a woman jumping into the canal in an apparent suicide attempt. He is torn between a desire to end his problems and an urgency to live. The suicidal woman seems to have made her choice. But before she can drown, she is pulled from the water by a passing policeman.

Raskolnikov's emotions are in such turmoil that this incident has an enormous impact on him. Should he commit suicide? Should he go to the police station and confess? Rather than doing either, he returns to the scene of the pawnbroker's murder, for "an irresistible and inexplicable desire drew him on." The murder remains the central focus of his conscious and subconscious life.

If his behavior with Zametov seemed self-incriminating and mad, it is mild compared to the way he acts at the scene of the crime. He wants to know where the blood is, despite the fact that the apartment is being redecorated. He's astonished not to find the corpses and disapproves of the new wallpaper. He rings the bell, three times. When the workmen press him for his identity, he tells them to come to the police station, that he will tell them there.

He acts even more bizarre with the crowd gathered at the gate, identifying himself by name and taunting them about their suspicions of him. What possible motive can he have in behaving this way? Are we to think that he's gone off the deep end? Once more he escapes. But, ask yourself, how often can this happen before he's arrested?

With every intention of going to the police, Raskolnikov leaves the scene, but his attention is distracted by a large crowd, full of shouts and flashing lights.

CHAPTER 7

The dreadful carriage accident and the man dying in the street recall two scenes: Raskolnikov nearly falling beneath the horses in Chapter 2 and the attempted suicide of Chapter 6. But this victim will not escape from death. The man lying broken in the street is no stranger, either: it is Marmeladov. Repeating over and over, "I'll pay, I'll pay," Raskolnikov arranges to have the injured man carried home.

The house of death is a pathetic place. The ragged children and the distraught mother seem even worse off than they did a few days before. Katerina Ivanovna is tough and doesn't faint. She is beyond pity for her husband. She offers no consolation to him, but instead speaks sharply. She doesn't want him to ask her forgiveness, and she offers none. Nor does she hesitate to tell the priest that she thinks what Marmeladov has done to all of them is a sin. She doesn't put much stock in God, either.

Katerina Ivanovna's attitude toward her husband is unwavering; even his death does not change it. He asked for what he got, she insists. What did he expect? Her overriding concern is, what will she do now? You wonder if she has any feelings at all beneath her tough exterior, but, still, it is hard not to sympathize with her. Clearly, she has had a dreadful life, and much of it was Marmeladov's fault.

Sonia, however, is forgiving, and Marmeladov dies in her arms. Hadn't he known all along that his daughter loved him? For the first time in the novel, faith is affirmed.

Raskolnikov, who has watched the scene silently, tried to console Katerina by recalling how much Marmeladov loved her. More important, he offers her money for the funeral: the roubles that remain from his mother's generosity. Promising to come again, he rushes from the room.

NOTE: Can you figure out what prompts Raskolnikov's gift to the Marmeladovs? There has been evidence before that Raskolnikov is moved by suffering. But to give them nearly all the money he has seems astounding. Are we to admire him for his sacrifice? Or is it further evidence that he has lost the power to think reasonably? It's entirely likely that he himself couldn't explain what his reasons were.

As he leaves the Marmeladovs, Raskolnikov feels rejuvenated—like a man who had been condemned to death and then unexpectedly reprieved. (Remember that this image has special relevance for Dostoevsky. He knew what it was to be reprieved from death.) But before we discover the source of this miracle, Polenka, Sonia's ten-year-old step-sister, catches up with him, wanting to know his name and where he lives. To show her gratitude and her willingness to love him, she hugs him and gives him a childish kiss.

Watching Raskolnikov with her, you'll probably find it hard to remember that he is a killer, or even the rude, self-centered person who always wants to be alone. The happiness he feels as he looks at her is something he doesn't understand, but he is touched when she cries. Even more, he is willing to ask her to pray for him. Dostoevsky has added some more mystery to his character.

Returning to the bridge where earlier in the evening the woman had tried to commit suicide, Raskolnikov is sure that his life is still before him. His illness is gone, and he's ready to reassert his strength. He's not sure how this transformation has happened, but he knows it has. The narrator cautions that perhaps he has concluded too quickly that his life did not die with the old woman. That doesn't occur to the jubilant Raskolnikov.

He is so excited that he decides to go to Razumikhin's party, but he is too weak to go in and join the festivities. He talks to his friend on the stairs. A slightly drunk Razumikhin tries to explain what Zosimov, Zametov, and even Porfiry think of Raskolnikov, but it comes out so muddled that neither Raskolnikov nor the reader is sure what anyone thinks.

Raskolnikov confides in Razumikhin that he has given the Marmeladovs all his money, but his explanation of the evening is confused. There is a clue, though, to his changed attitude: "I have been kissed by a creature who, even if I had killed anybody, would still . . . ." Even though he does not finish the explanation, it is clearly his sense of being loved that has made such an impact on him. You'll discover that loving and being loved are important to Raskolnikov and to Dostoevsky's ideas about salvation.

Dizziness sweeps over Raskolnikov, and Razumikhin helps him to his room. But panic returns. There's a light under the door. The murder isn't behind him after all. But it isn't the police who wait for him. His mother and his sister throw themselves on him in ecstasy. The sudden release of tension is too much for Raskolnikov. Once again he faints.

PART III

CHAPTER 1

Raskolnikov comes to quickly, but the shock of his family's presence overwhelms him. He looks so ill that his mother is terrified. All he can say to them is "Go home. . . ." It's hardly the greeting they expected.

As if everyone weren't unhappy enough, Raskolnikov blurts out his anger to Dunya. He categorically forbids her to marry Luzhin. Wanting desperately to salvage the situation, she tries to postpone the discussion, but he won't stop. He insists that he won't let her sacrifice herself for him; he refuses to consider that she has any other motive for marrying Luzhin. His ultimatum—Luzhin or me—follows them as they leave. By this time even the patient Razumikhin has had enough. He shouts: "You must be out of your mind."

NOTE: Everyone who has come in contact with Raskolnikov since the murder resorts to explaining his behavior as madness. You're probably tempted to agree with them. But Dostoevsky doesn't intend insanity to be an excuse for Raskolnikov's behavior.

While the unhappiness of the reunion lingers, the mood of the chapter changes dramatically as Razumikhin takes the women to the sleazy hotel Luzhin has chosen. It is almost funny to watch him fall in love with Dunya. He chatters on, in a tipsy euphoria. But his romantic haze doesn't prevent him from carrying out his responsibilities; he is very definitely in charge.

Pulcheria Alexandrovna and Dunya are deeply upset by Raskolnikov's behavior. Their worry is never far from the surface. But Dostoevsky distracts our attention from their misery by his description of Dunya. In particular, we learn that she resembles her brother, not only physically but also emotionally. This connection between them becomes increasingly important as the story continues. For one thing, it is one way in which Raskolnikov's appealing qualities are illustrated.

If Raskolnikov has failed them, Razumikhin does all he promised. He settles them in and returns almost immediately to report that Raskolnikov is sleeping. Within an hour he brings Dr. Zosimov to reassure them about the patient's condition. It's clear he's becoming very important to the Raskolnikov women. It's a role he treasures.

"Some suspicions of mental disturbance" and "some indications of monomania" are the doctor's diagnosis. He advises them to avoid upsetting Raskolnikov the next day, when they try another reunion.

NOTE: This emphasis on madness works several ways. Labeling Raskolnikov's behavior monomania protects him from being a murder suspect. His obsession with the crime is explained as a mental disturbance. Also, if he is mentally sick, his family and friends are willing to forgive a lot of obnoxious behavior. You have to consider, though, whether labeling someone mentally disturbed really protects him. Maybe it is the labelers it really protects—from facing the truth.

CHAPTER 2

Raskolnikov is the main subject of conversation in this chapter, but he never appears. You discover what Razumikhin, editing discreetly, tells Raskolnikov's mother and sister about him and what they have noticed themselves.

Razumikhin has begun the day in a fit of depression because he feels he has disgraced himself by being so presumptuous and "disgusting" with Raskolnikov's sister and mother. Despite his worst fears, however, he is greeted enthusiastically at the hotel and treated as a dear and trusted friend. While he tries to spare the women's feelings, he is direct and honest about Raskolnikov. It would be hard to find a clearer analysis of the problem than his: "It is as if he had two separate personalities, each dominating him alternately." On the good side, Raskolnikov can be warm and generous. But the bad side seems to have the upper hand. He is depressed, hypochondriacal, cold, unfeeling, egotistical, and self-centered. This explanation probably confirms our own observations, and it articulates Dostoevsky's interest in dual, or double, personalities.

Dunya, grateful for his honesty, suggests that perhaps what her brother needs is a woman's love. But Razumikhin isn't sure that would work either, because he isn't sure Raskolnikov is capable of loving anyone.

Pulcheria Alexandrovna admits that he has always been difficult. Capricious and cranky are the words she uses. She is distraught and she admits she has always been afraid he might do things no one else would think of. A recent example was his inexplicable engagement to the landlady's daughter. Razumikhin has no explanation for that interlude, except to say the girl was "plain . . . sickly . . . and odd." Raskolnikov's mother is honest enough to say she'd glad the girl died.

The conversation then turns to Luzhin. Razumikhin admits that Raskolnikov was rude to the man. This time he doesn't use illness as an excuse. And he admits he is ashamed of his own behavior.

But Raskolnikov and Razumikhin's assessment of Luzhin's character is about to be reinforced. The women show Razumikhin a letter in which Luzhin demands that Raskolnikov not be present when he makes his much delayed visit that evening. Worse, you can recognize a deliberate lie. The letter describes Raskolnikov giving away his twenty-five roubles to "a notoriously ill-conducted female . . . on the pretext of funeral expenses." You know perfectly well what really happened.

NOTE: Once again, Dostoevsky has given you more information than any of the characters have. He expects you to use it to draw your own conclusions about Luzhin.

As the confused women prepare to meet Raskolnikov again, they are slightly better prepared to cope with him. And you have a little more information with which to figure out what he will do next.

CHAPTER 3

The enthusiastic opening, announcing Raskolnikov's recovery, describes his physical health, not his emotional well-being. Dr. Zosimov watches him carefully, trying to analyze his behavior. So does the reader. And, amazingly, he seems to be in control of himself.

For the first time, he seems able to carry on a conversation and even show a little mocking wit when the doctor says everything will be fine if he just goes back to school. Even more important, there are real flashes of affection that delight his mother and Razumikhin. She, in particular, thinks how wonderful he is. But remember that in the past Raskolnikov has found her love smothering and intolerable. The feeling that this reconciliation can't last forever is too clear to ignore.

NOTE: In this scene everybody is talking at cross purposes, and the characters' thoughts overlap and blend into what they actually say. The result is an atmosphere of confusion and tension. Dostoevsky uses this technique to show just how complicated the relationships between these people are, and how difficult it will be for them to have a true reconciliation.

Raskolnikov admits to his mother his inexcusable action in giving away her money, a flash of honesty that reveals his better side. In particular, he puts into words the real pity he feels for suffering people. This enforces the reader's sense of his humanity.

His vulnerability comes through too. "Are you afraid of me?" he asks Dunya. But when he reassures his mother that there will be plenty of time for talk, he realizes immediately that it's a lie. He'll never be able to talk to anybody honestly ever again. He is so depressed he nearly walks out of the room.

When he tries to explain the relationship he had with his fiancée, he admits he was attracted to her because she was sick, and says he would have liked her even better if she had been lame or deformed. This strange attitude is left hanging in the air. We don't understand Raskolnikov any better after he describes his engagement, but we do have a clearer sense of just how disturbed he is.

The burning issue of the visit is still unsettled, but Raskolnikov will not ignore it any longer. With an insincere apology for his bluntness the evening before, he again demands that Dunya must choose between being Luzhin's wife and being his sister. She can't be both. She insists it is her own business. But he will not accept that.

NOTE: Raskolnikov is convinced that Dunya is marrying for his benefit, and he hates her sacrifice. Is this another example of his egotism? Or does he really have Dunya's happiness at heart? Dostoevsky leaves the answer up to you. One of the things that should influence your decision is what you know about Luzhin.

The similarities between brother and sister are clear in their quarrel. She is as stubborn as he. And with a barb that only Raskolnikov and the reader can understand, she shouts at him: "If I destroy anybody it will be myself and nobody else . . . I have not killed anybody!"

Raskolnikov almost faints, but he pulls himself together. Dunya insists he read the letter from Luzhin, which only makes the situation worse. Raskolnikov insists the man is illiterate, but more, he claims that Luzhin has lied about him. Because you know that Raskolnikov is telling the truth, much of the rest of what he says has credibility too. If Raskolnikov is right about Luzhin being a liar, and you know he is, perhaps you should believe the other things Raskolnikov says about him, too.

Dostoevsky builds up the suspense about how this problem will turn out. Dunya insists that Raskolnikov be present at the interview with Luzhin. And she makes clear that she has already made up her mind. We will have to wait for her decision, and so will Raskolnikov.

CHAPTER 4

As if the tension were not high enough, Sonia Marmeladova walks into the room. She is shy and timid, and for a moment Raskolnikov doesn't recognize her. She isn't dressed for the street, and seems poor and very young.

Her humility fills him with pity, and he treats her gently. You can see another crack in his egotism, as you did when he gave Katerina Ivanovna the money and when Polenka gave him a hug. Sonia has a mission, and she's eager to finish and leave. She has come with an invitation to Raskolnikov, for the funeral and the dinner afterward, events, she points out, that his money is paying for. Her stepmother implores him to come, she says. Her own invitation is unspoken.

Though she is eager to leave, Raskolnikov insists that she stay. Despite her occupation, he deliberately introduces her to his mother and his sister, embarrassing all of the women. But Dunya and Pulcheria Alexandrovna are touched by Sonia's gratitude and her demeanor. The girl is clearly astounded that anyone as poor as Raskolnikov would have been so generous to her family. Dunya even manages to bow politely as they leave the room. For just a brief moment, Raskolnikov is serenely happy, convinced that life is worth living.

Before Raskolnikov will allow Sonia to leave, he draws Razumikhin aside to tell him that he wants to see Porfiry Petrovich, the investigator in charge of the murder, to reclaim the pledges he had left with the pawnbroker. Razumikhin is delighted and urges that they go at once.

A provocative little incident distracts our attention for the moment, before we join Raskolnikov and Razumikhin on their way to visit Porfiry. Sonia is conscious of being followed by a stylishly dressed man when she returns home. He stays behind her, and follows her up the stairs to the same floor. He expresses amazement at the coincidence that they live next door to each other. But we are left completely in the dark. Who the man is and what he wants is a mystery. Remember the coincidence though: many critics find it a significant weakness in the novel that the unfolding of the plot depends on such an unlikely event.

After this digression, we rejoin the men on their way to visit Porfiry. Razumikhin's excitement about the visit grows by the minute, and he can't disguise how delighted he is to hear about his friend's dealings with the pawnbroker. For him, it is clear, Raskolnikov's obsession with the crime now has an explanation.

NOTE: Dostoevsky's technique may be a little hard for you to follow here. What Raskolnikov is thinking and what he is saying are both expressed in dialogue form. You have to recognize which is which. The juxtaposition emphasizes the division in his personality. Further, we learn about his determination to use his brains in order to control the situation.

Unaware of his friend's internal dialogue, Razumikhin falls into Raskolnikov's deliberate deception. Just as Raskolnikov intends, they enter Porfiry's house laughing boyishly.

CHAPTER 5

Raskolnikov, as we have seen, deliberately sets up a jovial atmosphere at the beginning of the conversation with Porfiry Petrovich. But he is unable to control the tone of the rest of the meeting, because he has met his match. He has a specific purpose in coming, but Porfiry has another purpose in keeping him there.

To begin with, Raskolnikov is upset to find Zametov in the room. Have Zametov and Porfiry been discussing Raskolnikov's incriminating behavior in the tavern? It's reasonable for us—and Raskolnikov to assume so. Although Porfiry is a small, stout fellow who doesn't seem very commanding, his eyes reveal his power. It doesn't take long for Raskolnikov to decide "He knows." The truth is, he probably does.

Raskolnikov continues his act, behaving as he thinks he ought to, in order to keep himself from being suspected. But every once in a while, Porfiry throws him for a loop. For example, he's known all along that Raskolnikov left pledges at the pawnbroker's, and he is careful to say that Raskolnikov is the last one to inquire about them.

For a moment, Raskolnikov's self-control cracks; he curses himself and lets his anger show. Once more, what Raskolnikov is thinking is plainly spelled out. He is disturbed to realize how much Porfiry knows. And he has reason to be.

The subject of the afternoon is crime. The first theory discussed—one that Razumikhin dismisses as nonsense—is the socialists' view. Crime, they say, is a protest against social injustices. If the economic system were fair, this theory says, there would be no crime.

Porfiry complains that Razumikhin's not giving a fair account of the idea, but Razumikhin is adamant. According to him, a theory that does not consider human nature as a cause of crime is nonsense. Porfiry insists, though, that environment does have a lot to do with crime.

NOTE: Because so much modern theory about crime adopts Porfiry's view, we tend to accept his idea. As a result, Porfiry seems even more logical and thoughtful to us. You may consider Razumikhin's opinion that evil people cause crime old-fashioned, but remember that it's the view Dostoevsky supports.

But it's Raskolnikov's views that Porfiry wants. He says that he's read an article that Raskolnikov has written, called "Concerning Crime." Taken by surprise, Raskolnikov admits that he hadn't known it was in print. But he's even more amazed that Porfiry knows who wrote it, because it wasn't signed. Clearly, Raskolnikov's fear of the investigator's persistence is justified.

It comes as no surprise to us that Raskolnikov's concern in the article is the psychological condition of the criminal and the illness that accompanies crime. We already know that he's fascinated by this idea. He's given a lot of thought to how a criminal will act when a crime is committed. He's told us that already.

But Porfiry has other things on his mind. Isn't it true, he asks, that the article claimed that some men have the right to commit crimes? Does Raskolnikov really believe that the law should not apply to certain "extraordinary" people?

Without denying the overall idea, Raskolnikov insists that he expressed it a little differently. There are several elements of his theory:

1. An extraordinary man does have the right, within himself, to "overstep" the law if his ideas require it. Raskolnikov explains that many of these "ideas" may help humanity, and he uses the example of the scientists Newton and Kepler. If people had stood in the way of their disseminating their ideas, they would have had the right to "remove" those stumbling blocks.

2. Men who make new laws are always transgressors. To make a new law, you must break an old one. Raskolnikov insists there is nothing new in this idea, and he is essentially right. The examples he gives are Lycurgus, Solon, Mahomet, and Napoleon.

3. There are two categories of people, ordinary and extraordinary. The extraordinary ones are those who have the right to overstep the law, based on the greatness of the idea they wish to expound. However, Raskolnikov hastens to add that not many extraordinary people get away with their actions.

NOTE: While the merit of Raskolnikov's ideas about extraordinary people is not debated by the group, you should try to come to terms with his ideas yourself. Are they insane? Immoral? Realistic?

Porfiry prefers to taken an entirely different approach. When Raskolnikov ends his explanation by saying that in his mind men have equal rights "until we have built the New Jerusalem . . . ," Porfiry asks if he believes in the New Jerusalem, in God, in Lazarus. This introduction of religious themes seems out of place, but it is not. Belief in Lazarus, in particular, which means belief in the miracle of the dead returning to life, in the Christian idea of resurrection, is crucial to the resolution of Raskolnikov's crime, and of the novel.

But having asked the question, Porfiry makes another leap. This time he asks, in a mocking tone, how you can tell an extraordinary person from anybody else. Raskolnikov chooses to ignore the mockery and answer the question. It is no problem, he insists, because anyone who acts as if he is extraordinary and isn't is no threat. He will punish himself.

Raskolnikov picks up Porfiry's mocking tone, but the chief difference between the debaters is that he is deadly serious, while Porfiry is not. To torment him a little more, Porfiry suggests a practical application of the theory. What if someone did commit a crime? But Raskolnikov is not to be outdone. Society has methods, like exile and prison, he says, to deal with criminals. And if they get caught, it serves them right.

Porfiry presses further: What about the criminal's conscience? Raskolnikov reponds that a man who has a conscience will suffer if he believes he's done wrong. If he feels pity for his victim, he will suffer. Further, he says that truly great men experience great sorrow as a consequence of their actions.

But it is the final question that is the most pointed. Porfiry asks if Raskolnikov considers himself an extraordinary man, and Raskolnikov responds, "Very likely." Their dialogue is tense. "Doesn't that tempt you to crime?" the investigator asks. "If I had done so, then of course I should not tell you," the murderer answers.

Razumikhin, who has listened in disbelief to the entire interview, is depressed, sensing that there is more to Raskolnikov's illness than he had ever imagined.

But Porfiry isn't finished. Trying to trick the weary Raskolnikov, he asks if he had seen the painters the night he was at the pawnbroker's. But of course they were there only the night of the murder. Razumikhin catches him in this trick, and points it out in a surly tone. He and Raskolnikov leave, gloomy and depressed.

NOTE: This astounding interview is important not only for the provocative ideas it presents and the insight it gives us into Raskolnikov's mind, but also as the beginning of Porfiry's strategy to trap Raskolnikov into confessing. You may find yourself returning to this scene to prepare for essay questions or to gather ideas for a writing assignment.

CHAPTER 6

Razumikhin and Raskolnikov discuss the meeting with Porfiry. Each is upset, but for different reasons. Razumikhin accepts the fact that Raskolnikov is a suspect; he admits the police have been suspicious, but he is furious about it. Raskolnikov, on the other hand, is cocky. They don't have any physical evidence, he's sure, so they can't pin anything on him.

When they get to the hotel where they are to meet the women, Raskolnikov can't bring himself to go in and face them. Nor can he tolerate his friend's companionship any longer. "Do *you* want to torture me as well?" he demands in despair.

NOTE: Raskolnikov's ability to put up a good front, to pretend to be in control, breaks down in front of those people who know him best. That may show that he feels guilty for lying to them. Of course, another way to look at it is that he is afraid that, because they know him so well, they will be able to see right through him and discover that he is a murderer.

Raskolnikov rushes home. Panic has struck again. Suppose there is some shred of evidence after all that can link him to the crime! If there is, he's finished. But of course there isn't anything left behind the torn wallpaper. Relieved, he leaves his room, but what follows is so bizarre that he soon comes rushing back to the only place he feels secure, a room his mother has described earlier as a "coffin."

The strange experience is an encounter in the street with an unknown man. The man has been asking for him by name. When Raskolnikov demands what he wants, the man says "Murderer!" Raskolnikov, weak-kneed and chilled, asks who is a murderer. With a smile of "triumphant hatred" the man replies, "You are!" And then he simply disappears.

The man's identity is a mystery. Some readers have even wondered if he is real, or simply a figment of Raskolnikov's imagination. But his impact is very real, and you'll run into him again before too long.

Secure in his room, Raskolnikov again tries to sleep, his customary escape. Disconnected and incoherent images flash through his mind. Conscious of his physical weakness, he curses himself as a failure. He is no *real* ruler, to whom all things are permitted. Nothing proves that to him more than his disgusting, insignificant victim. How could he have thought she was worthy of killing?

His confusion is evident. On the one hand, he
asserts that he was killing on principle, and that he
was eager to "overstep all restrictions . . . ." On the
other, he says he acted because he didn't want his
mother to go hungry. How can those very different
motives be resolved?

One thing he tries is self-criticism. Maybe he's been
pretending to act for good reasons; maybe only the
selfish ones were important. He insists he tried for an
appropriate victim, and that he meant to take only
what he needed. He decides, though, that he's the
biggest louse of all, bigger than his repulsive victim,
because he knew beforehand he'd fail.

NOTE: Raskolnikov's attack on himself raises an
interesting idea: did he commit murder to prove to
himself that he's worthless, as a form of self-destruc-
tion? That makes as much sense as anything else to
some readers. They argue that everything he does is
to punish himself for his failures.

But his greatest anger is reserved for the dead
pawnbroker. Nothing will make him forgive the old
witch for putting him through this anguish. He's
blaming her for how he feels after murdering her!

Raskolnikov is so worked up that he becomes totally irrational. He turns against his family. How he
hates them! He hates the old woman too. If he had a
chance, he'd kill her again! But his raving stops when
he thinks of Lizaveta, the one he didn't mean to kill,
the one who reminds him of Sonia. He falls asleep
with the meek and gentle Sonia on his mind.

Again he dreams, a horrible dream that reveals his
extreme vulnerability. He follows the mysterious
accuser to the pawnbroker's flat, where everything is

as it was the night of the murder, except a fly—an ugly, seemingly insignificant pest—buzzes. He senses that the old woman, huddled under a clock, is afraid. He has come to kill.

When he hits her over the head, she laughs, and doesn't seem affected by the blow at all. Whispering and laughing come from the bedroom. He hits her madly over the head, but the more he hits, the more she laughs. He tries to run away, but the entrance is full of people watching him. Screaming, he wakes up. Just then an unknown man walks into the room. Is this a nightmare too?

Ten minutes pass. Finally, Raskolnikov can't stand it any more. "What do you want?" he demands.

"I am Arkady Ivanovich Svidrigailov," the man answers.

NOTE: From here to the end of Part VI, the lives of Raskolnikov and Svidrigailov are intertwined in many ways. Dostoevsky makes the similarities between them very clear (something Svidrigailov loves to point out); but the differences are even more important. Watch the parallels and intersections of their lives closely.

PART IV

CHAPTER 1

The dramatic entrance astounds Raskolnikov. But, for the moment, Raskolnikov's problems are put aside. Svidrigailov has come on very particular business.

NOTE: The beginning of this chapter demonstrates the novelist's technique of building up a moment of tension and then defusing it so that more details can be added to the plot. In that way, the novel is a kind of emotional roller coaster for the reader as well as the participants.

Svidrigailov, Dunya's former employer, wants to enlist Raskolnikov's aid in seeing Dunya again, now that his wife is dead. When he doesn't get much response, he demands, "Am I a monster or am I myself a victim?" That is the critical question, not only about Svidrigailov, but about Raskolnikov as well. The parallels have begun.

When Raskolnikov accuses him of being responsible for his wife, Marfa Petrovna's, death, Svidrigailov insists his conscience is clear. That sounds familiar too. Part of his explanation makes him particularly offensive, though. Women, he claims, like to be affronted and outraged, even beaten a little now and then.

Notice, though, that in some ways he is more tolerable than the self-righteous Luzhin. He is candid about himself and observant of others. He explains that he used to be a gambler, and that Marfa Petrovna paid off his gambling debt; in turn he married her. His most striking characteristic is his total boredom. He has tried many things, and has no desire to do them again. The only new idea he has is for a "journey," which is not defined. But suicide is surely implied.

The ghost of Marfa Petrovna haunts Svidrigailov. Raskolnikov tries to tell himself that Svidrigailov is crazy, but the latter keeps insisting that the two of them have a great deal in common. Most readers agree—as Dostoevsky wants them to.

Raskolnikov doesn't want to think about that possibility. It's too close to what he fears is the truth. The more Svidrigailov talks, the clearer the similarities become: he too is repulsed by Luzhin and convinced that Dunya is selling herself for the family's good. He wants to make her a present of 10,000 roubles so that she won't have to go through with the marriage. Raskolnikov is astounded.

Svidrigailov's explanation seems to make sense. He did Dunya harm; now he wants to do good. He has no ulterior motive, he insists, and may, in fact, soon marry someone else. But he does want to see Dunya one more time.

The reader is not sure how to answer the question Svidrigailov asked in the beginning. Is he a scoundrel or a victim? Both seem possible, at this point.

CHAPTER 2

Raskolnikov is troubled and confused by Svidrigailov's visit. He senses a threat to Dunya, but that is only part of a greater mystery. He is frightened that Svidrigailov has been another apparition, a hallucination. Since Razumikhin saw him on his way in, that is unlikely, but, still Raskolnikov is not sure. "Perhaps I really am mad." he worries.

Razumikhin tries to cheer him up, but it doesn't do much good, especially as they encounter Luzhin on the way to the fateful eight o'clock meeting.

Luzhin has a new enemy to attack, and he does so with relish: Svidrigailov is a degenerate, depraved man who has come to St. Petersburg with evil intentions, Luzhin says. He tells two tales of suicide that he blames on Svidrigailov. But you already know that Luzhin is a liar, especially when he thinks it will serve his own cause. Whether he is telling the truth now, you can't tell. Dunya seems inclined to doubt him.

Raskolnikov tells her what Luzhin has omitted from the Svidrigailov story: that Marfa Petrovna left her 3000 roubles in her will, and that Svidrigailov wants to see her. But Raskolnikov doe not say what Svidrigailov really has in mind.

Luzhin behaves in typical fashion, and Dunya is very angry with his pomposity and self-importance. He even rouses the timid Pulcheria Alexandrovna to anger. She accuses him of having lied about the money given to the Marmeladovs. Haughtily, he prepares to leave, but they aren't finished with him yet. Challenged, he can't control his nastiness.

With no regret, Dunya tells him to get out. When he threatens never to return, she assures him that she hopes he doesn't. What outrages him most is that he has spent money on them, but, as Pulcheria Alexandrovna points out, it was precious little. Like the spiteful person he is, he can't resist trying to get in the last word, slandering Dunya's reputation. But as he is forced to leave, his anger is centered only on Raskolnikov.

NOTE: In thinking about the guilty people in the novel, notice that Dostoevsky makes it easy for us to compare Raskolnikov with Svidrigailov and with Luzhin by placing the chapters describing these men close together. Which one of them do you find the most repulsive, the most monstrous? What are the things that he says or does that make you feel that way?

One note of caution though: Dostoevsky allows you a lot of independent conclusions, but he does have a very definite opinion about these men and what happens to them. You have to hold your final judgment until all the pieces are in place.

CHAPTER 3

Luzhin is a self-made man. He loves his money and his power. And he loves himself. What he wants most of all is to find a wife to fulfill his sexual fantasies, a woman who, because she has been poor, will look upon him as her lord and savior. How she will humble herself before him! He can't wait! And, if he chooses wisely, she can even help him climb a little higher on the social ladder.

But now all of his dreams are in shreds. His optimism tells him that tomorrow everything will be all right. In his egotism he is unable to admit that his hopes are destroyed. He doesn't understand how that could possibly have happened. Is it possible to feel sorry for him? Does Dostoevsky provide any details that seem to you to justify pity or sympathy?

When Luzhin leaves, everyone is elated. They're serious for a moment, though, as Raskolnikov tries to explain Svidrigailov's offer of 10,000 roubles. He realizes the man is disturbed, perhaps even a little crazy, but he's not prepared for Dunya's response. The idea of seeing him again panics her; his blatant sexuality terrifies her.

But even the thought of Svidrigailov can't depress them for long. Razumikhin enthusiastically proposes that they invest some of their new-found capital with some that he will borrow to start a publishing business. Dunya catches his excitement, and even Raskolnikov joins the planning.

Then, without a word of explanation, in the middle of the conversation, Raskolnikov is suddenly ready to leave. He tells them all that he loves them and insists that they must leave him alone. "Otherwise I feel I shall begin to hate you. . . ." Nothing can change his mind, and he implores Razumikhin to protect his mother and sister. With the mysterious words "I will come . . . if I can," Raskolnikov walks away.

As the two men part, staring at each other, Razumikhin suddenly recognizes with a shudder the truth about Raskolnikov's guilt. He will ask no more questions. Raskolnikov leaves.

This chapter and the one before are a little reprieve; for a while the murder has slipped into the background. But it can't be avoided for long.

CHAPTER 4

Raskolnikov goes straight to Sonia. Her room, like his, shows the profound poverty in which she lives. The yellowish wallpaper recalls the decadence and disillusion discussed earlier. Raskolnikov's preoccupation makes it hard for him to focus, and he's vague, even confused. Once more, his instability is the most predictable thing about him.

But he does pay attention to Sonia, and his compassion for her distracts him from his own misery. Her ability to feel pity for others, especially her wretched stepmother, is boundless. The more Sonia explains how desperate and muddled the older woman is, the more obvious it becomes to Raskolnikov (and to us) that she doesn't want to face the inevitable. He tries to force her to face reality, though, and admit that Katerina Ivanovna is incapable of caring for herself or the children, and that Sonia herself will have to support them—a hopeless task.

His honesty seems cruel to Sonia, and intolerable. "God will not allow it," she insists. That is her chief defense against all of the terrible possibilities that Raskolnikov describes. Raskolnikov torments her: "Perhaps God does not exist."

But his cynicism can't endure for long in the face of her suffering. Or maybe it's just that he has an emotional need for her full attention. He falls to the ground and kisses her feet, the classic Christian gesture of humility and adoration.

Painfully, he explains that he honors her because of her great suffering. It is true, he says, that she is a sinner and her greatest sin has been to suffer *in vain*. All of his bitterness and disbelief pour out: you are helping nobody, he insists. All you have suffered is a total waste. Why don't you commit suicide?

Though she doesn't understand everything he says, she doesn't seem surprised at that question. Has she asked herself the same thing, Raskolnikov wonders. What's stopping her? He seems to have forgotten his own decision, not long before, to go on living.

His thoughts run wildly on. What choices does she have? Suicide? Insanity? Corruption and debauchery? How can she go on with her life the way it is? He clings to the idea that she is insane. That explains everything. You might find some ironic humor in his conclusions. Isn't calling him crazy the only way other people can explain Raskolnikov's behavior?

Out of the blue, he asks, "Do you pray a great deal to God?" His scorn is obvious. This time he has gone too far, and Sonia indignantly tells him he is not worthy to question God.

Suddenly, Lizaveta's New Testament is in his hand, and he asks Sonia to find him the story of the raising of Lazarus and to read it aloud. (The story, about Jesus' raising Lazarus from the dead, is found in the Gospel of John, Chapter 11.)

As she reads the story, with its message of hope and salvation, she has a hard time but keeps on reading. She is nearly ecstatic as she reads of the miracle of

Lazarus coming back to life. Then she can read no more. Silent minutes pass.

Raskolnikov finally interrupts, changing the subject once more: he has come to tell her something and he must do it. He has deserted his family. Sonia is all he has left. Sonia is frightened and confused. He insists that they are both lost souls and must suffer together. But he is raving; she can't figure out what he's talking about.

His parting words disturb her even more: tomorrow, if he comes, he will tell her who killed Lizaveta.

Sonia is upset but also strangely happy. It never occurs to her who the murderer is. But unknown to both of them, their conversation has been overheard by her fascinated new neighbor, identified for the first time as Svidrigailov. This is the coincidence Dostoevsky foreshadowed in Part III, Chapter 4.

CHAPTER 5

We begin to understand Raskolnikov's curious comment—to both Razumikhin and Sonia—that he will return *if he can*, when we discover that the first thing he does the next morning is visit Porfiry Petrovich. As he waits for the interview, he thinks he's going to be arrested. But as the minutes go by, he convinces himself that the accusing stranger must not have reported him to the police.

His frustration and anger grow. He dreads another encounter with Porfiry. He fears that he will betray himself. Just then Porfiry sends for him. The investigator has won the first round in the war of nerves. But he, too, is nervous and ill at ease.

NOTE: Most of this chapter is dialogue—the narrator doesn't tell you much. So you've got to pay attention to the *tone* of the conversation as well as the words and make your own interpretations.

Raskolnikov can't resist the urge to bait and taunt his adversary. Porfiry in turn torments him. And while Porfiry keeps the upper hand, Raskolnikov's sense that something strange is going on persists. You can feel it too. Look at all Porfiry's remarks. He didn't behave this way before.

One of Porfiry's methods is flattery, complimenting Raskolnikov on the brilliance of ideas he hasn't expressed, and deferring to his knowledge of law. And he shares his own philosophy of catching criminals with his visitor. Some criminals, he says, should not be arrested right away, or they won't incriminate themselves. The psychological value of keeping the criminal on edge helps the investigator enormously, Porfiry laughs as if he were sharing some enormous joke with Raskolnikov.

In a war of nerves, the criminal will always lose, always betray himself, Porfiry claims, because he is psychologically unable to resist incriminating himself. But Raskolnikov is neither fooled nor defeated. He resolves to resist, to beat Porfiry at his own game. By keeping silent, holding his anger inside, he seems to encourage Porfiry's chatter. But the chatter isn't pointless; nearly every comment is a barb.

At last Raskolnikov can stand it no longer. He tells Porfiry he knows he is suspected, and *insists* that if there is any evidence he be arrested immediately. He refuses to be tormented. He hardly seems to realize that he has no choice in the matter. He is appalled, too, that the investigator seems to know everything he's done, including the return visit to the old lady's house. Porfiry says that if Raskolnikov doesn't calm down, he will go genuinely crazy. But he lays yet another trap, by telling a story of a man who imagines himself guilty when he is not.

The tricky questions continue, and Raskolnikov, beside himself, confronts the investigator: either Porfiry is lying, or he is making fun, Raskolnikov says. Porfiry insists that he's telling the truth, and that his chief source is Raskolnikov himself. But Raskolnikov is not appeased. He demands to know if he is suspected of the murder. When no answer is given, he is beside himself with rage, pounding the table with his fist. "Don't play with me! Do not dare . . . ," he rages.

But Porfiry is only amused, and says that he has a little surprise in store, if Raskolnikov would like to unlock the door. Furious again, Raskolnikov demands that Porfiry reveal his information. But the real surprise astounds them both.

CHAPTER 6

Everything is in wild commotion, with Porfiry the most outraged of all. A pale, strange man has walked uninvited into the office and fallen to his knees despite Porfiry's orders to take him away.

"I am guilty . . . . I am the murderer!" the painter Nickolay confesses. Porfiry is in a stupor. He is so astounded by this turn of events that he nearly forgets that Raskolnikov is standing in the room.

Trying to usher Raskolnikov out with the explanation that he shouldn't be there, Porfiry has to admit his admiration for the daring that Raskolnikov shows in asking if he isn't going to see Porfiry's "little surprise."

Porfiry insists that they will see each other again, but Raskolnikov, made bold by Nickolay's unexpected confession, feels like a new man. For the moment his battle with Porfiry is a tie. Raskolnikov is shaken, though, for he knows that Porfiry knows too much for him to be completely safe. But for today he is free, and he will go to the funeral dinner and see Sonia.

But this incredible day has one more surprise: the man who had accosted him in the street walks into his room. The stranger is full of contrition for having accused him, and for having gone to Porfiry. Even more, he is appalled at the way Porfiry baited Raskolnikov while the stranger waited behind the closed door as the "surprise." He begs forgiveness for his slander and his spite.

Raskolnikov is elated, but bitter, too. The bitterness is at his own cowardice, which had almost given him away.

NOTE: The mysterious, unnamed character whose accusation is such a psychological blow to Raskolnikov and such a boost to Porfiry's case is one of the more perplexing characters in the novel. As we noted earlier, he doesn't seem realistic. Nor does his explanation seem to justify the accusation he made. Should we conclude that this character is just a clumsy plot device that Dostoevsky used to speed up the confrontation? Some readers think so. Or does he demonstrate that irrational actions, like Raskolnikov's return visit to the flat, doom criminals?

PART V

CHAPTER 1

The scene shifts in this part, but it's still the same day, the day of Marmeladov's funeral.

Luzhin has not given up his hopes of a reunion with Dunya, although he has admitted to himself that he was a fool for being so stingy. But rather than blame himself, he blames Raskolnikov for all of his problems.

We learned earlier that Luzhin is staying with Lebezyatnikov in the same building where the Marmeladovs live. The two don't get along very well the day of the funeral. Lebezyatnikov is offended that Luzhin is counting large sums of money in his presence; he thinks Luzhin wants to make him feel poor and insignificant. One thing Lebezyatnikov doesn't lack is words. He uses more words to say less than anybody in the novel.

NOTE: Lebezyatnikov's conversation is peppered with allusions to 19th-century political thinkers, most of whom advocated radical changes in society that Dostoevsky rejects and mocks. There is political satire in the novel, but it is difficult for readers who aren't familiar with 19th-century Russian social history. It's probably fair to say that includes most readers today. What is important to pick up here, and in the other places where such issues are raised, is that Dostoevsky has no patience with the revolutionary ideas, or with the characters who advocate them. So when anyone raves on about reform, you can be pretty sure Dostoevsky portrays him as a fool.

Even Lebezyatnikov's foolish ideas seem tolerable in contrast to Luzhin's hateful and suggestive remarks about Sonia, whom he wants to meet. In a deliberate foreshadowing, the reader learns that some of Luzhin's money is left out on the table, but it's only mentioned in passing. If you miss it, the following events, and Luzhin's subsequent accusation of Sonia in Chapter III, may be confusing to you.

Asking Lebezyatnikov to stay in the room, Luzhin greets Sonia warmly. In a deliberately pleasant—and totally phony—way, he inquires about her family. But he calls Katerina Ivanovna a fool for setting her heart on a pension, and for spending what little money she has on a funeral dinner. He offers Sonia ten roubles, the most he says he can spare. Murmuring her thanks, Sonia flees.

For once Lebezyatnikov is impressed with his guardian's behavior, and assures him that he has *seen* all. Soon he is off again, on another of his tirades of social reform, but Luzhin is too excited to listen.

NOTE: While the description of Luzhin doesn't use psychological terms, Dostoevsky is portraying him and his motives—just as he has Raskolnikov—by what the character himself says and does. The author wants you to form your own conclusions as you watch Luzhin in action.

CHAPTER 2

The pathetic ritual of the funeral dinner, which Katerina Ivanovna can't really afford and yet feels compelled to hold, ends in nearly total disaster. The disturbed and irrational widow has grasped this occasion as one to prove that she has not always been poor and must be respected. Her tendency to exaggerate the slightest detail makes her appear ridiculous, but her advancing illness is pathetic.

NOTE: The trauma of illness and poverty is a powerful message of the novel, and one that Dostoevsky describes brilliantly. You can't escape it.

Her most foolish idiosyncracy is her mockery of the landlady Amalia Ivanovna. Like many other characters in the novel, the landlady is considered offensive because she is German (a prejudice of Dostoevsky's), but that hardly seems to explain Katerina Ivanovna's constant tormenting of the woman. The landlady has the upper hand, though; it is her house. She screams that they must move out, and insults Sonia in the bargain. As Katerina Ivanovna leaps for her, Luzhin appears on the threshold.

CHAPTER 3

In Katerina Ivanovna's usual style, she totally misjudges the situation. Calling to Luzhin for protection, she is rudely rebuffed. He has come, he says, to talk to Sonia.

Deliberately he addresses the girl by the wrong patronymic, either to show his disdain or to rattle her; worse, he accuses her of having stolen a hundred-rouble note. If she confesses immediately, he promises not to carry the matter further.

Everyone is dumbfounded. Sonia, stunned, whispers that she doesn't know what he is talking about. Given the opening he needs, Luzhin launches into a tirade of slander and accusation. Stricken, the terrified Sonia tries to return the ten roubles he had given her.

But the mocking looks on the neighbors' faces show that the others believe him. Luzhin threatens to call the police.

Katerina Ivanovna, out of control, shrieks at him and at the landlady who has joined the accusation. "I am not meek!" she screams at them. It is a deliberate repetition of the word Dostoevsky has used to describe Sonia and Lizaveta, the saintly sufferers. Luzhin brushes her aside, ready to search the girl, but Katerina Ivanovna herself empties Sonia's pockets. The hundred-rouble note, folded small, falls at her accuser's feet.

Frenzy follows. The landlady howls; Sonia sobs her innocence; and Katerina Ivanovna has her finest hour, for she praises her step-daughter's honesty and self-sacrifice. She begs the crowd—particularly Raskolnikov who has stood silently by—to defend Sonia.

Even Luzhin is moved to pity by her pathetic agony, and offers to let the matter rest. After all, the poor destitute girl had a good motive in her theft, he says.

"What a foul trick!" "How despicable!" Lebezyatnikov speaks from the doorway, staring at Luzhin, barely able to control his fury. The startled Luzhin tries to defuse the situation by questioning Lebezyatnikov's sanity. But the accuser is totally sane and completely in control. He has watched the entire scene from the doorway, dumbfounded. He can't figure out what Luzhin is trying to do, for he had seen Luzhin himself secretly slip the folded note into Sonia's pocket.

Once more the room explodes in frenzy. Luzhin tries desperately to salvage his control, but Lebezyatnikov won't back off. His labored eloquence persuades his listeners that he is telling the truth, and Luzhin's efforts are wasted. Once more he tries slander to carry the crowd with him.

At last Raskolnikov steps forward. He is calm and self-assured—a very different person from his usual self. He will explain it all. He recounts, in explicit detail, the story of the broken engagement and Luzhin's innuendoes about Sonia's character. He charges that this attempt to discredit Sonia is in reality meant to destroy Raskolnikov's credibility with his mother and sister. Lebezyatnikov confirms this interpretation by remembering that before Luzhin asked to see Sonia, he had wanted to know if Raskolnikov were among the guests.

Down but not out, Luzhin pushes off the menacing crowd, sticking to his story that he has been robbed and maligned; within half an hour he has left the building. And he's left the story. We never hear any more about him.

Sonia's vindication can't ease her agony. She is too aware how vulnerable she is, how close to disaster she has come. Barely in control of herself, she flees.

And the landlady, outraged by her own "suffering," insists that the exhausted Katerina Ivanovna move out at once. Out of control, the miserable widow rushes away, looking for the "justice and truth" she desperately believes she will find. The room becomes bedlam.

Raskolnikov sets off after Sonia. Surely she can no longer believe that God is protecting them all! he thinks.

NOTE: Luzhin's accusation is one of the most dramatic confrontations in the novel. But Dostoevsky gives us more than excitement. Think about what Luzhin has done—or tried to do. For his own selfish (and offensive) ends—to get Dunya to marry him— he has planted evidence and maligned an innocent person. Yet he feels no remorse. He has no conscience. His only concern is for himself.

Compare him to Raskolnikov. Which man is more of a criminal? Of course, Luzhin hasn't murdered anyone. But he has tried to destroy an innocent person.

CHAPTER 4

Preoccupied with his need to tell Sonia who killed Lizaveta, and with his fears for the future, Raskolnikov follows her home. Her greeting makes it clear that she has been expecting him.

When she hears that Katerina Ivanovna has been evicted, her first impulse is to go to her. But Raskolnikov persuades her to stay—in part because he needs her himself, and in part because her willingness to suffer for others, despite her experience with Luzhin, drives him crazy.

He poses a hypothetical question. Suppose she could decide if a person were to live or die. What would she do? But Sonia has no patience for things that are not real, and she is upset that Raskolnikov seems to be trying to trap or torment her again.

For once, he yields to her objection and admits that what he really has come for is her forgiveness. For a moment an irrational flash of hatred—like his hatred for his family—fills him, but he sees the love in her face and all his anger vanishes. He knows that he must confess. The moment has all the tension of the moment of the murder: the beating heart, pale face, and speechless lips.

His torment is clear to her, and she tries to comfort him. But he impatiently insists that he has come to tell her who killed Lizaveta.

Insisting that killing Lizaveta was an accident, that the killer had not meant to harm her, Raskolnikov makes Sonia look at him until the dreadful truth dawns on her.

Fighting desperately within herself to deny what she now knows, Sonia finally throws herself on her knees before the tortured Raskolnikov. "What have you done to yourself?" she implores, holding him tight.

He can't believe her reaction. How could she kiss someone like him? But her pity is genuine and honest. Pathetically, almost childishly, he asks if she will forsake him. But Sonia will follow him anywhere, even to prison.

NOTE: A critical difference between Raskolnikov and Sonia comes out in this disjointed conversation. She is distressed that he did not come to her before the crime. Clearly she thinks she could have kept him from it. But for Raskolnikov, this was the only way. Without the crime, he never would have come to Sonia at all.

The more Sonia thinks about the murder, the more perplexed she is. How could he have done such a thing? She wonders if he was robbing to help his mother, but Raskolnikov finds it impossible to explain his motives. Her confusion grows. How could a man who gave away his own money to strangers be a robber?

He admits that he doesn't know how much money he stole. That only makes her more baffled. And it is no wonder, for as Raskolnikov talks he doesn't make his points very clearly. He asks again if she will stick by him, and admits that he has asked her to join him in his suffering because he is unable to bear it alone. He craves reassurance.

At last he is able to say that he killed because he wanted to be a Napoleon. But of course Sonia has no way of knowing what he means. Raskolnikov explains his anguish that the only test he could put himself to was such a meaningless one. But it was his only chance, he explains. When Sonia finds this explanation difficult to understand, he offers a vastly different one. He killed for the money so that he would not have to take any more from his poor mother, he says. And he admits that killing the old woman was "wrong."

Yet a moment later he insists he killed a louse, not a human being. When Sonia disputes that, he says the most honest thing of all: he doesn't know what the truth is anymore. He had many reasons, but he has no words to express them.

When he tries again, he suggests that he is evil, vile, vindictive . . . a whole chain of terrible qualities. And perhaps he is even a little crazy, he admits. He could have stuck it out at the university and found jobs to support himself, he realizes. But he isolated himself, and in his isolation resolved that the only people who mattered were those who dared to be masterful. Power exists only for those who will take it. He killed because he wanted to dare, to have the courage to be a great man, he claims.

Sonia is appalled. He has done the work of the devil, she says. But for Raskolnikov that is too easy an answer. He insists that he murdered for himself, to test whether he had the right to be a great man. But he has failed. He really is only a louse. And that is why he has come to Sonia.

He pleads with her to tell him what to do, but when she insists that he confess to the police, he is thunderstruck. Her belief is that he must suffer and atone, but he refuses.

Suddenly, he has a new thought. Perhaps he really is a man after all. Maybe he has just been too hard on himself. Maybe there is still fight left in him. He won't give up. He knows they have no evidence. Even if they arrest him, he will prevail. But the grief Sonia feels for him is a weight on his soul, for he senses the responsibility that her love imposes on him. Is he better or worse off than he was when he came?

She asks him to wear her cross, but he is not ready yet. Sonia is confident that the time will come when he will ask for it and they will pray together. There is good reason to think she is right, for hasn't Raskolnikov changed enormously because of his contact with her? But on the other hand, having to explain himself seems to have given him new courage. Something must shift the balance.

Just then Lebezyatnikov comes to the door.

CHAPTER 5

Katerina Ivanovna has gone completely crazy, Lebezyatnikov tells them. She has taken the children into the streets to dance and sing and beg money from passing strangers. Sonia rushes out, intent on helping her desperate family.

Raskolnikov returns to his own room, feeling dreadfully alone and yet full of pity for Sonia. He knows he's added to her sorrows, and he's disgusted with himself for having made her unhappy.

While he broods, his sister enters. She too loves him, Raskolnikov recognizes. She has come to say that she knows he is suspected, and that if there is anything she can do he need only ask for it. But his only response is to praise Razumikhin, and Dunya is suddenly very afraid.

NOTE: Many readers feel that one of Raskolnikov's biggest errors is not putting more confidence in his sister and in her ability to understand and forgive. Perhaps he feels ashamed in front of her, as he doesn't with Sonia. Dunya, after all, is not guilty of anything, so Raskolnikov may believe that she can't understand and forgive guilt in others.

As Raskolnikov mulls over his plight, Lebezyatnikov rushes in. Again he is the messenger of doom. Sonia has been unable to get her dying stepmother off the street. The situation is desperate. Raskolnikov goes to help. The scene makes all that has gone before pale. A more pathetic destruction of human dignity is hard to imagine, as the dying mother and her starving children dance in the streets. Sonia can't make her stop, nor can Raskolnikov. Her insane fantasies run on, interspersed with the children's songs.

When a policeman tries to intervene, Katerina Ivanovna loses all control and falls, exhausted and dying, in the street. They carry her wasted body to Sonia's room; her delirium increases. But she rejects the idea of calling for a priest. She insists that she has no sins, and that God owes her something for all the suffering she has gone through. Many readers agree with her.

Her death leaves her orphaned children terrified, but Svidrigailov—who, we suddenly recall, lives in the room next to Sonia's—insists that he will make all the funeral arrangements. Even more, he will place the children in a good orphanage and leave an annuity for each of them so that Sonia will not have to worry about them. He makes a particular point to tell Raskolnikov that he is using the money he wished to give Dunya, but Raskolnikov is immediately distrustful.

And well he should be. For Svidrigailov makes clear that he has overheard Raskolnikov's confession, and that knowledge must be reckoned with.

NOTE: Part V is in many ways the most depressing section of the novel, but Dostoevsky also uses it to hint at the story's hopeful resolution.

PART VI

CHAPTER 1

Raskolnikov seems, even to himself, to be living in an unreal world. But even in that haze he realizes two things: One is that Svidrigailov poses a threat to his safety. Another is that Sonia loves him. He must come to terms with these two facts. He almost wishes there were another crisis for him to deal with, something to snap him out of his confusion.

NOTE: Ask yourself if you feel sympathy for Raskolnikov in this chapter. The novel seems to shift you back and forth from sympathy to disgust with him, and you have to decide which feeling is finally stronger in your own mind. Ask yourself, too, how you think Dostoevsky wants you to feel. Because the narrator never says, directly, how you ought to react, you've got to recognize the clues he gives you.

When Razumikhin comes to talk, he says he has to know if Raskolnikov is sane or not. Of course, it doesn't seem the smartest thing to ask Raskolnikov, but Razumikhin is desperate. He can't understand why Raskolnikov is acting the way he is. If he's insane, at least that's one way to explain it.

Razumikhin is especially upset because he knows what Raskolnikov's behavior is doing to his mother and sister. This has been a problem all along, because Raskolnikov has resented having to worry about them.

The other problem for Razumikhin is trying to figure out what kind of trouble Raskolnikov is involved in. He's relieved that Nikolay confessed to the murders and ashamed that he suspected Raskolnikov of the crime. If it's hard for you to imagine yourself as a killer, think about how you'd feel if you suspected a friend of yours was guilty of some awful crime. Razumikhin still suspects that Raskolnikov is involved in some sort of desperate action, but he is easily distracted at this point by Raskolnikov's mention of Dunya's feelings for him. As he leaves, he's a happy man, with thoughts of love on his mind.

After his friend leaves, Raskolnikov tries again to figure out what to do. He is astounded when Porfiry shows up unexpectedly. After days of being terrified of just such a visit, suddenly he feels absolutely calm.

CHAPTER 2

The visit begins in an unusual way, considering that a police investigator is talking to a man he knows is a killer. Porfiry begins by saying he owes Raskolnikov an apology for trying to trick him. He hopes they can be honest with each other. He claims that he admires Raskolnikov enormously and that he thinks they're very much alike. He feels sorry for Raskolnikov, he insists, and then he explains how he became suspicious of him. But Porfiry's a crafty fellow, and he doesn't tell any more than he absolutely intends to. He does say, though, that Raskolnikov's article was particularly important in directing his suspicions at its author. He also makes a point of telling Raskolnikov that his room was searched, that his conversation with Zametov in the tavern was incriminating, and that his laughter on the first visit to the police station provoked suspicion. Porfiry hasn't missed a thing. If this were a detective novel, he would be the hero.

He's also got an explanation for the painter's confession; the young man is a religious fanatic, and his sense of being a sinner is so profound that he feels he should suffer. But there were too many errors in the man's confession, Porfiry tells Raskolnikov, and it's perfectly clear that the painter isn't guilty at all.

What really rattles Raskolnikov is that Porfiry seems to know exactly what happened, and doesn't hesitate to say that Raskolnikov is the killer. And even when Raskolnikov denies it, Porfiry insists he's guilty.

But Porfiry also admits he has absolutely no evidence. If Raskolnikov doesn't confess, there isn't a case. So before any evidence is found, before he is forced to arrest him, Porfiry wants Raskolnikov to admit the crime. It will be easier on them both, he claims. As you might expect, Raskolnikov is scornful of that idea. But Porfiry is determined. He offers a deal—plea-bargaining we'd call it today. If Raskolnikov confesses, Porfiry promises the sentence will be reduced. When justice is served, Porfiry maintains, Raskolnikov will be able to regain his self-esteem— and find God's forgiveness too.

NOTE: Despite his scornful refusal to confess, Raskolnikov is very upset. The more Porfiry explains Raskolnikov's own behavior to him, the more depressed Raskolnikov gets. At last someone does really understand the complex ideas in his mind! And what good does it do?

But we can see a crack in Porfiry's pose of absolute assurance that Raskolnikov will confess. He can't resist—although he does it very awkwardly—asking him, if he does decide to commit suicide, to please leave a note saying where the loot is.

CHAPTER 3

From the conversation with Porfiry, Raskolnikov heads straight for Svidrigailov. After all, he could be a damaging witness in any trial. But as Raskolnikov hurries toward the meeting, he is conscious of a new feeling, one of being completely tired of the whole business. Worn down by tension is another way to express the way he feels. For some reason he doesn't really understand, he feels drawn to Svidrigailov.

NOTE: Remember all the earlier hints from the narrator and from Svidrigailov himself that Raskolnikov and Svidrigailov had a lot in common? Dostoevsky clearly wants the reader to think about the ways in which the two men are alike and the ways in which they're different.

As he hurries along, a dreadful thought occurs to him: what if Svidrigailov tries to use what he knows in order to get what he wants from Dunya? The old urgency to protect her wells up in him. If he has to confess in order to save Dunya from that awful man, he'll do it! And while it never occurs to Raskolnikov what a revealing decision this is, you may be pleasantly surprised by it. Is it possible that he really loves his family more than he loves himself?

"I shall kill him," he decides. Should we conclude from his words that Raskolnikov is really more dangerous to society than Porfiry thinks? There isn't really any evidence to think the threat is serious. The desire to kill occurs to many people, but most don't do it. Raskolnikov killed before to test his theory, not in rage or self-defense. If anything, this threat makes him seem more normal.

Quite by accident Raskolnikov spots Svidrigailov in a tavern and joins him. As they talk, it is clear that one enormous difference between them is in their attitudes toward sex. Raskolnikov is puritanical, and disgusted with the idea of Svidrigailov's "debauchery." Svidrigailov's excuse is that without women, he'd be so bored he'd have to kill himself.

NOTE: It is interesting that sexuality is associated only with Svidrigailov and with Luzhin. Neither Dunya and Razumikhin's nor Sonia and Raskolnikov's relationship has an explicit sexual component. Many readers think this is the result of Dostoevsky's own puritanical attitudes toward sex.

Sex doesn't interest Raskolnikov, but suicide fascinates him. "Could you shoot yourself?" he asks Svidrigailov.

The subject tortures Svidrigailov, and he doesn't want to talk about it. He doesn't want to be alone, either, so he implores Raskolnikov to stay. Clearly he's a man in deep emotional trouble.

NOTE: Raskolnikov and Svidrigailov do a lot of talking, but they don't really communicate. Each is in his own world of private torture. We know more about what Raskolnikov is thinking than we do about Svidrigailov's thoughts. But at this point it is still difficult to see what the two men have in common, since they seem so different in tastes, attitudes, and behavior.

CHAPTER 4

Svidrigailov tries to explain the circumstances of his love for Dunya, and as he does it he ironically compares it with Raskolnikov's relationship with Sonia. It was Dunya's pity for him, and her desire to "save" him from his sins that made him love her, he says. That, of course, is similar to Raskolnikov's situation with Sonia. But the basis of Svidrigailov's love is sexual passion, an element that does not play a part in Raskolnikov's feelings.

Dunya was frightened—even repelled—by his passion, Svidrigailov says. But he was consumed with desire for her. Finally, he offered to buy her love: he would give her everything he had if she would run away with him.

The conversation convinces Raskolnikov that Svidrigailov still desires Dunya, but the mysterious man has a shocking announcement to make: he's found a new bride, and he's getting married. His bride is 16 years old, and he's quite taken with the response she has shown to his attentions. Raskolnikov is repelled by the sensuality that excites Svidrigailov. And Svidrigailov, for his part, seems to take great delight in telling stories that he knows will get Raskolnikov riled. When they part, Raskolnikov's suspicions that Svidrigailov is still in pursuit of Dunya remain strong.

NOTE: Perhaps the key to the chapter is Svidrigailov's disclaimer: "I am only a sinful man!" Raskolnikov, on the other hand, is a criminal, and yet he does not consider himself sinful. Has he any right to judge the behavior of anybody else?

•

CHAPTER 5

Raskolnikov confronts Svidrigailov with his suspicions, but Svidrigailov is not intimidated. Indeed, he uses the opportunity to remind Raskolnikov that he knows about the murder. And he urges him to run away to America. Svidrigailov is more cunning than Raskolnikov; he manages to throw the young man off his trail. He is alone in time to meet Dunya for the final time.

She is suspicious of him still, and insists they conduct their conversation in the street. He acts straightforward, but the reader learns immediately that he is lying. He says that Sonia is at home when he knows she is not, and so persuades Dunya to come to his room; further, he leads her to believe that his landlady is in the next room, which is also a lie. Dostoevsky is making it clear that this is a man who can't be trusted, especially when his sexual desires are involved.

Though she is frightened, Dunya is also determined to understand what Svidrigailov has suggested in his letter to her: that her brother is guilty of crime. She insists that it is a lie, but Svidrigailov doesn't pull any punches. He says he heard Raskolnikov's confession to Sonia.

Obviously he paid detailed attention, for he's able to repeat not only her brother's practical reasons—his need for money—but also Raskolnikov's theory about extraordinary people. Curiously, like Porfiry Petrovich, Svidrigailov seems to understand Raskolnikov, and even to observe that what is bothering him most is humiliation. It's been a blow for Raskolnikov to have to admit that he is not a man of genius, Svidri-gailov explains.

Dunya, on the other hand, is horrified; surely her brother must have a conscience! Why hasn't he con-fessed? Many readers share Dunya's reaction.

Svidrigailov, taking advantage of her distress, offers to make everything right. He will get tickets, provide the money, take care of getting Raskolnikov out of the country. Once again he's trying to make himself indis-pensable. But Dunya will have none of it. Desperately she tries to leave, but the doors are locked. Notice how carefully Svidrigailov, in contrast to Raskolnikov, executes his plan. No open doors for him!

Once more Svidrigailov tries to assure her that everything will be all right—but at what cost! The price he asks is Dunya's love and submission. Abject in his begging, he swears that if she will have him, he will do anything she wants. He nearly loses control of himself in his eagerness for her. Trapped, Dunya calls for help, but, as we already know, there is no one to hear.

Dunya is revolted by the idea of Svidrigailov touch-ing her. As Svidrigailov realizes that, a frightening change comes over him. He threatens her. He has her just where he wants her. How can she resist when she knows that her brother's life is at stake? And after all, he says, she did come to his room, didn't she? What did she think would happen?

Her indignation doesn't affect him. If anything, it pushes him further. You can buy your brother's free-dom, he pleads. Who could blame you for that?

But Dunya has come prepared. She pulls a revolver from her purse, and points it directly at her tormen-tor. Svidrigailov is astonished. And he's even more astonished when she shoots, grazing his forehead with the bullet.

If the scene between them were not so potentially tragic, it would be funny. Clearly he is capable of seizing the gun, of overpowering her in an instant. But for some reason he doesn't do it. He waits.

She fires again, but the gun misfires. She has a horrible realization, a deep insight into this strange man: he would rather die than let her go.

NOTE: The intensity of the scene between Dunya and Svidrigailov is heightened by the fact that the narrator is telling us about both their thoughts at once. Usually, in *Crime and Punishment*, one character or the other is stressed, but in this scene Dostoevsky wants us to see both Dunya's potential for violence and Svidrigailov's desperate efforts at self-control.

For a moment, Svidrigailov seems to have won. Dunya throws down the gun, and he gently embraces her shaking body. But once more Dunya rejects his advances, begging him to leave her alone. When she insists she can never love him, he is a stricken man. Suddenly he hands her the key, saying, "Take it; leave quickly! Quickly! Quickly!" The terrible tone of his voice frightens her, and it should. He is barely able to control himself.

Think again of a comparison with Raskolnikov. Raskolnikov at least has Sonia to love him. Dunya despises Svidrigailov and he's forced to acknowledge that fact. All she leaves behind is her revolver, and Svidrigailov leaves the room with it in his pocket.

CHAPTER 6

In another of the astounding reversals of behavior that characterize Svidrigailov, he stops to see Sonia and gives her 3000 roubles because he doesn't want her to live as a prostitute anymore. And, he says, because he is going away, no one will ever know where the money came from, for she must never tell. Further, he warns her that Raskolnikov has only two choices: to confess and be punished, or to kill himself.

Despite his generosity, it is clear that something is very wrong with Svidrigailov, and his behavior fills Sonia with "vague and distressing forebodings." Clearly, Dostoevsky is warning us of approaching disaster.

Svidrigailov pays another visit and gives his fiancée and her impoverished family 15,000 roubles, with the rather thin explanation that he will be away for awhile and he wants her to have her wedding gift before he goes.

Having finished his errands, Svidrigailov goes, alone, to a seedy hotel and a tiny, dismal room. In this environment, so reminiscent of the garret where Raskolnikov lives, he's cut off from humanity. And, like Raskolnikov, Svidrigailov is lost in daydreams and nightmares. Thoughts of Dunya fill his mind; he remembers her pointing the gun at his head. The memory fills him with pity for her and profound unhappiness for himself.

As he falls asleep, he dreams that the mice with whom he shares the room are running over his body, and he wakes in horrified disgust. He falls asleep again and dreams he is in a beautiful garden full of flowers. Among the flowers is a beautiful young girl, with fair, wet hair and a bitter expression on her face. Svidrigailov recognizes her: the girl who committed suicide after he sexually abused her. How horrible! How repulsive!

In yet another dream, he pulls on his coat and goes out into the cold, rainy night. Then on an endless walk down a long hall he finds a child—no more than five—wet, shivering, and crying. Sobbing, the child is unable to answer his questions, and so Svidrigailov carries her to his room, undresses her, and puts her into the bed.

As he checks the child to make sure she is okay, she seems strangely flushed. But it is not fever as he suspects. As he watches her, suddenly she laughs, and tries to seduce him. Her face is no longer the face of a child, but the face of a whore. As the horrified Svidrigailov reaches out to strike her, he wakes.

He has seen, at last, his own decadence, and he is disgusted. There can be no salvation. So clutching Dunya's revolver, Svidrigailov goes out into the early morning and puts a bullet through his head.

CHAPTER 7

Once more Dostoevsky suggests, by the pattern of the novel, connections between events that in some ways seem unrelated. This chapter, immediately following Svidrigailov's suicide, begins with Raskolnikov on his way to visit his mother. This visit too is a farewell. And because he too has spent the night wandering in the rain, he looks especially disreputable.

NOTE: Dostoevsky suggests that the fury of the evening's storm has been in sympathy with the frenzy of Raskolnikov's mood, the "inward strife" that has plagued him. This literary device of having nature be responsive to human feelings is called the pathetic fallacy. In reality of course, nature doesn't respond to our moods, but people are comforted by the thought that it does.

Raskolnikov's mother tries desperately not to ask too many questions or to upset him. But the terror she feels wells up to the surface. Her transparent feelings don't anger him, though, as they have done before. He has come on a mission: to ask if she will always love him, no matter what happens. He also wants to tell her that he loves her very much and always has.

This is a new side of Raskolnikov. There is no arrogance, no cynicism, no bitterness in his tone. And when he asks her to pray for him, there is no mockery. Moved by his mother's agony at his situation, he is able to act like a son again.

When he returns to his room, he finds Dunya waiting for him. He is able to be honest and loving with her too. To quiet her fears, he admits that he spent the night wandering along the river thinking of suicide, but that he could not kill himself.

NOTE: Chapter 7 presents another scene in which you, the reader, know something that the characters don't realize yet: that Raskolnikov and Svidrigailov spent the same night resolved to kill themselves. And as we know, Svidrigailov did and Raskolnikov didn't. Dostoevsky wants us to figure out why, to understand how important love is in rescuing people from despair.

Raskolnikov tells us why he decided to go on living: he knew that if he killed himself it would be to save himself from shame. But his pride told him that he could survive shame. He has decided to give himself up.

It isn't because he thinks he's guilty of crime, he explains. He still rages against the idea that killing the old woman was a crime. She was such a louse, he exclaims, such an extortionist, that killing her was a favor to mankind. That's what his theory said all along.

He's giving up because he hates himself, he says, because he has to face the idea that he isn't extraordinary. His imcompetence as a bold man demands that he admit the killing. Maybe this way he will be able to salvage his pride.

Dunya tries, but fails, to convince him that his ideas about crime are wrong. He insists that he believes, more strongly than ever, that his theory is right. But he respects, maybe even admires, his sister's objections and tries to comfort her. At the same time, he rebels at the idea of punishment and wonders if he shouldn't have killed himself after all. He asks a question that troubles our judicial system even today: what good will twenty years in prison do?

NOTE: In one last moment of rebellion, Raskolnikov looks for others to blame for his predicament, but he is grasping at straws. He can't, with any justification, blame what has happened on the people who love him. But why *did* it happen? How did Raskolnikov reach the point of committing such a desperate act? In the novel, as in real life, the tangled web of causes and motivations remains, to some extent, a mystery.

CHAPTER 8

Raskolnikov's journey to confession takes him first to Sonia. Because she has been so afraid that he might commit suicide, she greets him first with joy. But the change in his mood astounds her. He has come for her crosses, he says.

Dostoevsky has chosen this image for a very specific reason. The cross, in Christian symbolism, is the ultimate sign of human suffering. But because it is

Christ's sacrifice for mankind that the cross reminds us of, it also has divine meanings. When Raskolnikov asks for the crosses—including the one that had been Lizaveta's—he is saying that he is asking for God's forgiveness and accepting the idea that he must be humble before that ultimate sacrifice, Christ's death.

But can he possibly be sincere? This is the man who has just insisted that he is not guilty of any crime. And Sonia realizes that there is something unnatural, even artificial, in his request.

He explains that he despises the crowds who will point their fingers at him, so he wants to humiliate himself. If he is no better than a criminal, he must punish himself for his failure to be an extraordinary man. The humility of the cross is a way to demean himself publicly.

NOTE: Whatever feelings Raskolnikov has for Sonia don't come to the surface in this scene. He doesn't tell her that he loves her, or even why he has chosen to use her method of confession. Some readers argue that he hasn't realized yet how important she is to him emotionally. He is still too concerned with himself and his own misery. Other, less sympathetic, readers think this is another example of Raskolnikov's selfish and repulsive personality. The only way he knows how to deal with people is to use them for his own purposes, they argue.

Insisting that he will go through with his confession alone, Raskolnikov leaves Sonia. Briefly, he wonders why he has gone to see her at all. His only answer is that he needed her tears; he needed to know that there was still somebody who cared about him. What a comedown, he sneers at himself, for somebody who had such a high opinion of himself!

As he moves through the crowd of drunks and beggars in the Haymarket, he is disgusted by them, but he follows Sonia's instructions. In the center of the crossroads (notice the repetition of the Christian image of the cross), he kneels down and kisses the ground. A crowd gathers around, sure he is drunk. He tries to say the words "I am a murderer," but can't quite get them out. As he moves away, he sees Sonia watching him.

In a flash, he recognizes that they will be together always, but it is hardly a moment of joy. He doesn't even acknowledge her presence. Instead, he goes directly to the police station, to the place where he had fainted two weeks before.

It's ironically funny that he meets the loud lieutenant, Ilya Petrovich, who tells him he has come too early if he wants to do any business. The officer rattles on, apologizing for having thought badly of the young man, oblivious to the reason for Raskolnikov's presence. The one startling piece of news in all of his chatter is that Svidrigailov has shot himself.

Raskolnikov is shocked; he suddenly realizes what we have known for a long time: the only person—besides Sonia and Dunya—who knows the truth about him is dead. Lightheaded, he makes his way out of the police station. He has been saved! he thinks.

But there, just outside the entrance, Sonia is waiting. Looks, but no words, pass between them. Raskolnikov turns back to the office.

"It was I who killed the old woman and her sister, Lizaveta, with an axe. . . ."

EPILOGUE

CHAPTER 1

When Raskolnikov confessed, he did a thorough job of it. He described the murder in such precise detail that the judges couldn't figure out why he was lying about not having counted the money. They couldn't believe he hadn't. But when they finally believed him, they concluded, ironically, that it proved the killer was temporarily mentally deranged. It seems that, just like today, temporary insanity was the "latest fashionable theory" about crime back then. This reminds us that some issues relating to crime haven't changed much in the last hundred years.

Raskolnikov does tell one big lie: he insists that he is sincerely remorseful, and that he committed the murder because he was desperately poor and needed the money to get on with his career. He also calls himself a coward and says that he has an unstable nature.

Dostoevsky doesn't explain this behavior, but leaves it to you to figure out. One thing you should remember is that he has mixed reasons for deciding to confess. All along, too, the idea that he is punishing himself has been a strong possibility. Perhaps publicly calling himself a coward satisfies a psychological need.

NOTE: The third-person narrator tells this part of the story very straightforwardly. He offers no insight into what Raskolnikov is thinking; he simply reports the facts. While in one way the trial is a crucially important part of the novel, it is also the least provocative. In Dostoevsky's view an impersonal system is making partially knowledgeable decisions. Here, at least, he is more critical of the system than of the killer.

Raskolnikov gets off with a relatively light sentence—eight years in Siberia. Many factors influence the court's decision: Raskolnikov's poverty, his mental instability, his confession. Porfiry's silence is important, too, for the court never knows that there was any suspicion against Raskolnikov. And his past is full of those strange, contradictory acts of goodness you saw, for example, in his treatment of the Marmeladovs.

His mother becomes ill almost immediately and dies, unable to cope with the uncertainty of her son's fate; Dunya and Razumikhin marry, and Sonia follows Raskolnikov to Siberia. Dostoevsky ties off all the loose ends.

If you imagined that any great change had taken place in Raskolnikov, you're in for a disappointment. He reacts to prison as you might have expected the "old" Raskolnikov to—he's sullen, indifferent, not interested in anything, not even Sonia's visits; in fact, he's rude to her. Finally, having alienated practically everybody except the long-suffering Sonia, he becomes seriously ill.

NOTE: There are many critics who think the book should end at this point. Raskolnikov is acting like himself, and so is Sonia, who—thanks to Svidrigailov—isn't a prostitute anymore. Realistically, they say, this is the logical conclusion to Raskolnikov's crime and punishment. But Dostoevsky has something very different in mind.

CHAPTER 2

Raskolnikov's illness, you soon discover, is once more psychologically based, just the way his reaction to the murder had been. He's still struggling with his humiliation; his illness is the result of his wounded pride—his loss of self-respect.

After all he's been through, he still believes he's not guilty of crime. He made a huge mistake, he does admit—but anybody could have done that. The thing he can't live with is that he caved in. You might even say the only thing he's sorry about is that he got caught. And it drives him crazy that the only person he can blame for that is himself.

Worse yet, he feels he's got nothing left to live for. He's convinced that if he'd been able to get away with his crime, he would have proved he was extraordinary. It's success, he believes, that determines what's right.

NOTE: In some ways it is tempting to accept Raskolnikov's argument about extraordinary people. History certainly shows that the victor makes the rules. And if you approve of the winner, you approve of the new way things are done. But Dostoevsky's point in this chapter is that Raskolnikov is wrong, and that the moment he decided against suicide his subconscious already knew it, even if his conscious mind didn't.

Raskolnikov does realize that he is hated and that Sonia is loved. But he can't understand what it is about her that makes people feel that way. Dostoevsky lets us see that the failing is on Raskolnikov's part, that his own inability to love and to care about people limits him as a human being.

Raskolnikov's illness comes at Easter, the Christian symbol of resurrection and rebirth. Like the sickness that struck him at the time of the murder, this one signals an important change in his life. Again, he has a frightening dream. But this time the dream has a very different effect.

His nightmare involves the entire world; everyone is infected with a strange disease. Those with the disease go mad, and consider their own ideas and convictions superior to everyone else's. Anarchy rules the world. Order dissolves. And those who are destined to lead the world into a new era can't be found. Raskolnikov can't rid himself of this image.

Then he finds out Sonia is sick, and he discovers a new feeling: he is worried about her.

When Sonia recovers enough to come to see him, a miracle has happened. Raskolnikov breaks into tears, and kneels before her. Instantly, she knows that he loves her and that they will have a future together. Dostoevsky's words are loaded with meaning: in their faces glowed "the dawn of a new future, a perfect resurrection into a new life." The Lazarus image recurs. Love has raised them from the dead.

But this love is greater than human, sexual love. It is the love of God that has shown through Sonia and her suffering. Loving her, Raskolnikov is also ready to love God. The seven years that remain on his sentence have a religious significance too, for seven is the number of creation, and the number of mystical union of man and God.

Dostoevsky ends the novel on a note of hope and joy. The past must still be expiated, but the future holds infinite promise.

NOTE: Not all readers can accept the ending of *Crime and Punishment*. Many, in fact, think that this chapter of the Epilogue is artificial and unconvincing—especially because of the miraculous transformation of the main character. They argue that, despite Dostoevsky's clear intention to write a novel with the message of salvation, he has not been convincing. His failure, they say, is the result of his extraordinary success in creating the character of Raskolnikov to begin with.

Your conclusion is up to you. Either you can accept Dostoevsky's view that salvation is possible—even for Raskolnikov—or you can decide that the real solution to the novel is in Chapter One of the Epilogue. That shows a bitter and hardened protagonist whose future is uncertain and not very promising. Whichever conclusion seems more believable to you is the one you can defend—using evidence of Raskolnikov's character based on your reading of the novel, and combining that evidence with what you know about life. Each side has been brilliantly defended by scholars and by other readers too. Remember, though, that Dostoevsky *intended* us to accept Raskolnikov's salvation.

A STEP BEYOND

Tests and Answers

TESTS

Test 1

1. The most obvious thing about Raskolnikov is _____ that he
   A. fears neither God nor man
   B. is a dual personality
   C. is worthy of redemption

2. The two contrasting aspects of Raskolnikov's _____ nature are presented by
   A. Dunya and Porfiry
   B. Avdotya and Luzhin
   C. Sonia and Svidrigailov

3. Raskolnikov is described as exceptionally _____ handsome in order to
   A. evoke the reader's sympathy
   B. establish a contrast with the ugliness of his crime
   C. validate Dostoevsky's theory

4. When Raskolnikov sees the desperate _____ situation of the Marmeladov family, he
   A. quietly leaves them some money
   B. counsels them on the need to change their ways
   C. vows to help them get back on their feet

5. Raskolnikov sees both Dunya and Sonia as _____
   A. prostitutes of a sort
   B. models of contemporary Russian womanhood
   C. victims of governmental indifference

6. "Do you understand what it means when you have absolutely no where to turn?" asks _____
   A. Sonia
   B. Razumikhin
   C. Marmeladov

7. In Raskolnikov's dream about the drunken peasant, he _____
   A. kisses the dead horse
   B. slashes the brute across the face
   C. throws the man under the horse's hooves

8. The actual murder of the pawnbroker is facilitated by the _____
   I. moving letter from Raskolnikov's mother
   II. crushing poverty which surrounds Raskolnikov
   III. fortuitous absence of the old woman's sister
   A. I and II only
   B. II and III only
   C. I, II, and III

9. The rationalization for the killing of old Alyona Ivanovna is that _____
   I. she was an evil person
   II. she had treated Raskolnikov's mother poorly

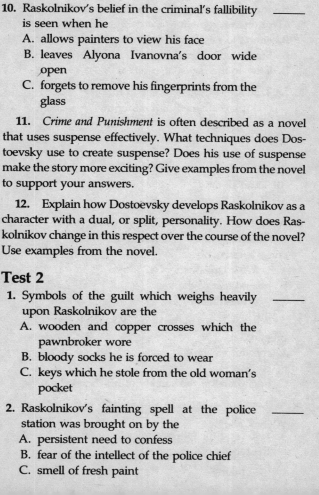

    III. her money could be used to help needy
       people
  A. I and II only
  B. I and III only
  C. II and III only

10. Raskolnikov's belief in the criminal's fallibility   _____
    is seen when he
  A. allows painters to view his face
  B. leaves Alyona Ivanovna's door wide
    open
  C. forgets to remove his fingerprints from the
    glass

   11. *Crime and Punishment* is often described as a novel
that uses suspense effectively. What techniques does Dostoevsky use to create suspense? Does his use of suspense
make the story more exciting? Give examples from the novel
to support your answers.

   12. Explain how Dostoevsky develops Raskolnikov as a
character with a dual, or split, personality. How does Raskolnikov change in this respect over the course of the novel?
Use examples from the novel.

Test 2

1. Symbols of the guilt which weighs heavily   _____
    upon Raskolnikov are the
  A. wooden and copper crosses which the
    pawnbroker wore
  B. bloody socks he is forced to wear
  C. keys which he stole from the old woman's
    pocket

2. Raskolnikov's fainting spell at the police   _____
    station was brought on by the
  A. persistent need to confess
  B. fear of the intellect of the police chief
  C. smell of fresh paint

3. Raskolnikov continually associates crime with _____
   A. punishment
   B. disease
   C. passion

4. Raskolnikov's empathy with the down-trodden and rejected is underscored by his _____
   A. prior engagement to a sick and ugly girl
   B. efforts to raise funds for Marmeladov's burial
   C. letter to the newspaper editor

5. Raskolnikov's crime is ironic in that _____
   I. it has chained him rather than freed him
   II. he makes no use of the money he stole
   III. it was inevitable that he would be caught
   A. I and II only
   B. I and III only
   C. II and III only

6. According to Raskolnikov's theory, the extraordinary man is allowed to commit a crime because he _____
   A. is free from conscience
   B. has no fear of the law
   C. is extraordinary

7. At least ten times in the novel, Raskolnikov is prepared to _____
   A. commit violence
   B. confess
   C. intellectualize the validity of his theory

8. Raskolnikov asked Sonia to read to him the Bible story of _____
   A. Jesus and the fallen woman
   B. the raising of Lazarus
   C. Judas' betrayal of Jesus

9. Raskolnikov identifies with Sonia because _____
   A. they have both transgressed against life
   B. her crime is as serious as his
   C. salvation is denied to both of them

10. Svidrigailov commits suicide after _____
   A. his showdown with Raskolnikov
   B. his dream about a little girl
   C. he learns of Raskolnikov's confession

11. The problem of crime and punishment has troubled people throughout history. Although Dostoevsky's *Crime and Punishment* takes place in 19th-century Russia, do his ideas have universal significance? Give examples that support your opinion.

12. *Crime and Punishment* is a novel of nightmares. Some are real and some are dreamed. Show how the dreams reveal the truth to their dreamers. Use examples from the novel.

ANSWERS

Test 1

1 B   2 C   3 B   4 A   5 A   6 C
7 A   8 C   9 B   10 B

11. To answer a question like this, think about the whole novel.

First, find examples of suspenseful scenes in the novel. Two of the most famous occur when Raskolnikov is in the pawnbroker's room at the time of the killing (Part I, Chapter VII), and when Dunya confronts Svidrigailov with the gun (Part VI, Chapter VI). Others occur throughout the novel, some in each part except the epilogue. You don't have to include all of them, but you should choose examples from different parts of the novel. The examples should be varied in subject too. For instance, the times when Raskolnikov thinks he's about to get caught are all alike in subject. So use only one of those.

When you've identified three different types of suspenseful scenes, describe each one. Mention when they occur, what they contribute to the story, what the language is like, and how the narrator's style or the dialogue reflects the tension. For example, when Luzhin tries to trap Sonia, Lebezyatnikov drops his long, complicated sentences and accuses him directly.

In your conclusion, explain how you, as a reader, reacted to the scenes, saying whether you think they added to your pleasure and understanding.

12. There are two different ways to answer this question.

The first, and perhaps easier, way is to explain, by using details from the novel, that Raskolnikov behaves in two distinctly different ways at different times. Sometimes he is hateful and cruel, as he is when he kills the women (Part I, Chapter VII), or when he tells Sonia her faith in God is useless (Part IV, Chapter IV). Other times he is generous and full of compassion, as he is when he gives the Marmeladovs money (Part I, Chapter II; Part II, Chapter VII), and when he tells his mother that he loves her (Part VI, Chapter VII).

To write a strong essay, you should decide which part of his personality seems more in control at different times—and why. Support your conclusions by describing what Raskolnikov says and does at different points in the novel. Remember to include episodes from the entire novel, including the Epilogue, in which Dostoevsky allows Raskolnikov's good side to triumph. Your conclusion might comment on whether you find that change believable.

The other way to answer the question is to compare Raskolnikov to some of his "doubles" or "foils." You can show how, on the evil side, he is like Svidrigailov, while, in his good moments, he can be like Dunya and Razumikhin. Note scenes in which Raskolnikov's similarity to an evil

character is pointed out—and scenes in which an evil character is used as a contrast to Raskolnikov. Your conclusion
should explain why it's significant that Raskolnikov lives
(like the good characters), rather than dies (like the evil or
weak ones).

Test 2

1 B   2 C   3 B   4 A   5 A   6 C   7 B
8 B   9 A   10 B

   11. In arguing that the novel's theme is universal, you
could point out that Dostoevsky touches on three critical
issues: the nature of crime, the psychology of the criminal,
and the way criminals can be punished.

a. Dostoevsky asserts the need for an objective moral standard, in which values are fixed. Explain what he says happens when an individual believes he can define his own
moral standard. You might discuss how the struggle
between individual ethics and society's values have frequently been a problem in many countries. Does Dostoevsky's concept of moral standards have any relevance
today?

b. The novel concentrates on the psychology of the criminal.
Dostoevsky describes various motives and reasons for Raskolnikov's crime, but none of them are ever really enough to
explain why a certain individual chooses to commit crime
and others don't. You could show, using contemporary
examples, that the psychology of the criminal is still a mystery, and that the issue of how much influence society has
on creating criminals is still alive.

c. Dostoevsky analyzes punishment that works. You can
argue that criminals who can't be rehabilitated are a major
problem in any country. But you must decide whether the
solution Dostoevsky proposes is workable or not, by spec-
ulating on how well Porfiry's methods of getting Raskolnikov to confess and ask for help would work on the typical

killer. Remember to point out that Raskolnikov is the only criminal in the novel who is rehabilitated. You can argue that Svidrigailov's suicide and Luzhin's arrogance prove that Raskolnikov is not a typical criminal.

12. Since both Raskolnikov and Svidrigailov are plagued by dreams, your answer ought to discuss both of them. For both men, Dostoevsky uses dreams to reveal the state of their minds and souls. And since Svidrigailov commits suicide while Raskolnikov is reformed, you should show what is different as well as what is similar in their dreams.

Because Raskolnikov is the protagonist and because his dreams are usually described in more detail, it's appropriate to start with him. He has three strikingly different dreams: the first is the one about the horse (Part I, Chapter V); the second is a mocking replay of the murder (Part III, Chapter VI); and the third is about a plague (Part VII, Chapter II). You can explain how each of them is related to the behavior that follows it, and describe what you think the dream means to the dreamer. Think about whether Raskolnikov sees himself clearly in each dream. You might argue that the dreams force him to act, or that rather they predict how he will act.

Svidrigailov's nightmare, just before he commits suicide (Part VI, Chapter VI), should be related to Raskolnikov's dreams. Explain how it is like them, and how it is different. Consider whether it reveals the truth about his behavior to his conscious mind so that he's forced to see himself as he really is.

In your conclusion, speculate on why you think Dostoevsky chose to use this device of dreams as a way to make the characters more complex. If you like, it would be appropriate to discuss modern ideas about the significance of dreams.

Term Paper Ideas

1. Compare Raskolnikov's victims, the pawnbroker and her sister. Why is it important that he kills them both? Why doesn't Dostoevsky develop either woman very clearly as a character?

2. Why is the novel so full of scenes of drunkenness, prostitution, and other seedy or decadent aspects of life? Explain how this environment is related to the crime Raskolnikov commits.

3. Compare the characters of Sonia and Dunya, the two most important women in the novel. Do they seem as realistic and powerfully drawn as the men?

4. Analyze the physical illnesses that plague the characters in the novel: Katerina Ivanovna, Raskolnikov himself, his mother, and other characters who are seriously ill. Are all the illnesses the same? What different things does being sick mean?

5. Look up some modern psychological explanations for deviant behavior. Do Raskolnikov and other "deviant" characters correspond to social scientists' attempts to explain criminal behavior?

6. Describe Porfiry Petrovich as a detective. What has he in common with other detectives in fiction and how is he different? You might compare him to Sherlock Holmes, for instance.

7. Identify and discuss the various Christian imagery and symbolism in the novel.

8. Why, in a novel with so many religious ideas, are there no churches and few clergymen? Research Dostoevsky's life to find out about his religious beliefs and about the organization of the Russian church during the years when he was writing *Crime and Punishment*.

9. Compare Raskolnikov to Shakespeare's Hamlet. They both have been described as men who experience the anguish of modern life.

10. What does Dostoevsky mean by alienation. Show the various ways that being alienated affect Raskolnikov.

11. Explain the contradictions in Raskolnikov's explanations for his crime. Does he really know why he has murdered the pawnbroker?

Further Reading
CRITICAL WORKS

Berdyaev, Nicholas. *Dostoevsky*. New York: The World Publishing Company, 1957. A series of essays on Dostoevsky and his world.

Frank, Joseph. *The Seeds of Revolt*. Princeton: Princeton University Press, 1976.

———. *The Years of Ordeal*. Princeton: Princeton University Press, 1983. The first two volumes of a life of Dostoevsky, generally recognized as a definitive study.

Gide, André. *Dostoevsky*. New York: 1926. The French writer's interpretation of Dostoevsky's life and work.

Guerard, Albert J. *The Triumph of the Novel*. New York: Oxford University Press, 1976. A work of highly acclaimed scholarship by a well-known critic.

Ivanov, Vyacheslav. *Freedom and the Tragic Life:* A Study in Dostoevsky. New York: Farrar Straus & Co., Inc., 1952. A highly respected and very readable classic.

Jackson, Robert L. *Crime and Punishment: A Collection of Critical Essays*. Englewood Cliffs, 1983. A recent work, with several essays of interest.

Jackson, Robert L., ed. *Twentieth Century Interpretations of Crime and Punishment*. Englewood Cliffs: Prentice-Hall, 1973. A valuable source of well known essays on the novel; part of a respected series of critical works for the general reader.

Margarshack, David. *Dostoevsky*. New York: Harcourt, Brace, 1963. A good introduction to the novelist.

Modern Fiction Studies. IV:iii (Autumn, 1958). An entire issue devoted to Dostoevsky, including a full bibliography up to 1958.

Molchulsky, Konstantin. *Dostoevsky: His Life and Work*, translated by Michael A. Minihan. Princeton: Princeton University Press, 1947. Many scholars consider this one of the best works on the novelist.

Simmons, Ernest J. *Dostoevsky, the Making of a Novelist*. New York: Vintage Books, 1940. A widely read and often quoted standard work.

Wasiolek, Edward, ed. *Crime and Punishment and the Critics*. San Francisco: Wadsworth, 1961.

_____, ed. *The Notebooks for Crime and Punishment*. Chicago: University of Chicago Press, 1974. The notebooks in which Dostoevsky recorded his plans for the novel.

_____. *Dostoevsky: The Major Fiction*. Cambridge: MIT Press, 1964. One of the most important critical works on the novelist. Important to any serious study of his work.

_____. "On the Structure of Crime and Punishment." *PMLA* LXXIV (March, 1959).

Wellek, Rene, ed. *Dostoevsky: A Collection of Critical Essays*. New York: Prentice Hall, 1962. Wide-ranging collection that includes Philip Rahv's article on *Crime and Punishment*.

Yarmolinsky, Avrahm. *Dostoevsky: His Life and Art*. New York: 1957. A general introduction relating his work and his life.

AUTHOR'S OTHER WORKS

1846	*Poor Folk, The Double*
1860	*The House of the Dead*
1861	*The Insulted and the Injured;*
	Notes from Underground
1866	*Crime and Punishment*
1868	*The Idiot*
1870	*The Eternal Husband*
1871	*The Possessed*
1875	*A Raw Youth*
1880	*The Brothers Karamazov*

Glossary

Alienation   Living as an "outsider," or in a state of isolation.

Civil Service (Russian)   An elaborate system of government jobs, divided into 14 ranks. Each rank had a distinctive uniform and social status.

Consumption   An old term for tuberculosis, a disease of the lungs that was a frequent and deadly killer until recent times.

Double, Doubling   A psychological term describing a character with two personalities, or two characters who represent different parts of the same person. In *Crime and Punishment*, Raskolnikov's different behavior patterns can be described as doubling.

Haymarket   A central crossroads, or square, of the slum district of St. Petersburg.

Icon   An image, picture, or representation of a saint or other Christian figure.

Lazarus   A New Testament figure, the brother of Mary and Martha, who were friends of Jesus. When Lazarus died, his sisters mourned for him, but Christ raised him from the dead after four days. This miracle is usually interpreted as a foreshadowing of Christ's own resurrection. In the novel, it suggests hope for Raskolnikov.

Monomania   Dr. Zosimov describes Raskolnikov's obsession with the murder as monomania. As a technical term for a pathological condition, it is no longer in use, but it is still used to mean a single-minded interest in one subject.

New Jerusalem   A term used by devout Christians to describe the way the world will be at the second coming of Christ. When Raskolnikov says he believes in the New Jerusalem, it means that he believes in God and in religious hope.

Napoleon Brilliant general who became Emperor of France and greatly affected European history. In 1812, he was defeated in his desperate attempt to conquer Russia, but he remained for Russians in general and Raskolnikov in particular a great hero.

Omniscient Narrator A storyteller who knows everything about the characters and shares that knowledge with the reader.

Pawnbroker Someone who lends money in exchange for personal property given as collateral.

Psychonym A name whose root indicates the personality or character of its bearer. For example, Razumikhin is a man of reason (razum= reason).

Rouble The Russian monetary unit.

St. Petersburg Known today as Leningrad, it was the Russian capital until 1918, and a cultural and literary center, too.

Shawl dance A dance characteristic of the education provided in upper-class finishing schools.

Siberia A vast area of Eastern Russia, used since the 17th century as a penal colony and place of exile for criminals.

Socialism A political philosophy popular in the 19th century as a way to eradicate some of the evils of society. The socialists' explanation of social injustice as a cause of crime was a theory Dostoevsky rejected.

Usury Lending money at exorbitantly high interest rates.

The Critics

The theme of alienation as the source of crime is the subject of this comment:

> *Crime and Punishment* was Dostoevsky's first great
> revelation to the world, and the main pillar of his
> subsequent philosophy of life. It was a revelation of
> the mystic guilt incurred by the personality that
> shuts itself up in solitude, and for this reason drops
> put of the comprehensive unity of mankind, and
> thus also out of the sphere of influence of moral law.
> A formula has been found for negative
> self-determination by the individual: the name for it
> was—isolation. Raskolnikov's incarceration within
> himself, which was the result of the supreme
> decision of his free will (a will cut off from the
> universal whole), finds its final expression in the
> crime he commits. The sequence is not from crime to
> self-incarceration, but the converse for from the latter
> arises the attempt to ensure the strength and autarky
> of the solitary personality—an attempt which, on the
> plane of external events, expresses itself as a crime.
> —*Vyacheslav Ivanov*, Freedom and
> the Tragic Life

Here's another perspective on the same subject:

> Raskolnikov never repented of his crime because
> he did not hold himself responsible for the murder.
> He had fancied that he could plan and carry out the
> deed, but when the time came to act, it was as if he
> were impelled by forces over which he had no
> control, by "some decree of blind fate." Man must
> suffer, he decides, because man, his intellect a
> delusion and its power demonic, trapped by his
> instinctive brutality and the conspiracy of his
> victims, does not will his destiny. "Not on earth, but up
> yonder," Marmeladov has cried out, "they grieve
> over men, they weep, but they don't blame them!"
> [Part I, Chapter 2] The aloneness of man is offended
> by the gods' refusal to blame what they cannot

blame, but once suffering, man's bondage, is
accepted man feels a part of something beyond
aloneness, feels no longer that he can be a god but
that he is part of the God that is "everything." The
revelation that comes to Raskolnikov through love
and humility "in prison, in *freedom*," is inevitable
because it is the obverse side, the *pro*, of the
will-to-suffering, the *contra*, that has been throughout
the entire novel his primary motivation.

> —*Maurice Beebe*, "The Three
> Motives of Raskolnikov," in *College
> English* XVII (December, 1955), p.
> 158.

Raskolnikov is a "double" character. Several critics have
commented on that aspect of *Crime and Punishment*. Here's
one:

Crime and Punishment is not only the first of
Dostoevsky's stories in which religion plays any part,
it is the first in which the double's dilemma is
worked out in terms of inwardness. It is also the
only novel in which a double is purged. Is
Raskolnikov really a double, and does he exhibit
affective and moral ambivalence? . . . Raskolnikov
does indeed wobble back and forth between the
claims of pride and pity. . . . he understands that the
interior battle is essentially between reason as an
instrument of the ego's desire for power and glory,
and the heart's sorrow for others. . . . He represses
pity as long as it gets in the way of the egoism that
his rational crime is fed by. But he never denies the
necessity of pity. "Pain and suffering are always
inevitable for a large intelligence and a deep heart.
The really great men must, I think, have great
sadness on earth." Not only does he never deny
pity, he is constantly tortured by his Titanic pride.
He has an instinct within him that solemnly
condemns him even while he refuses to listen. In
Raskolnikov too the contradictions exist side by side.
Repression only acts to elevate one side, it does not
make the other any less active. Time after time

Raskolnikov's pity produces works of compassion, charity, and self-sacrifice. What makes his simultaneity or doubleness look different is that his reason remains active on one level, and pity on another. . . . *Crime and Punishment* is the story of the half-conscious debate of inwardness rising slowly and surely to a fully conscious plane. Raskolnikov confesses to the police, not because he has failed or been caught, but because he knows he cannot resolve the torment of his questionableness or suppress the inward debate.

—*Ralph Harper*, The Seventh Solitude *pp. 50-51.*

Here is another comment on Raskolnikov and the concept of the ''double'':

Raskolnikov may act irrationally at times, but he is not mad nor even half-mad, and his creator never intended him to be mad. . . .

Raskolnikov is a typical Double. Dostoevsky makes this perfectly clear in Razumikhin's description of his friend in the novel. ''He is morose, gloomy, proud, and haughty; of late (and perhaps for a long time before), he has been mistrustful and depressed. He has a noble nature and a kind heart. He does not like to show his feelings, and would rather do a cruel thing than open his heart freely. . . .''

This ''alternating between two opposing characters'' is the most sustained feature of Raskolnikov's nature.

To the very end of the novel, and even in prison, the dualism of Raskolnikov pursues its relentless course. It is impossible for him to accept either path as the solution: the path of blood and crime to power or the path of submission and suffering to a Christ-like salvation. He loves and hates both, the meekness and submission of Sonya and the self-will and desire for power of Svidrigailov. Indeed, both these characters represent the extreme poles of his dualism and it is psychologically inevitable that he should be drawn to each of them.

—*Ernest J. Simmons*, Dostoevsky, The Making of a Novelist *pp. 142, 147, 151.*

NOTES

NOTES

NOTES